ACCORDION EULOGIES

ALSO BY NOÉ ÁLVAREZ

*Spirit Run: A 6,000-Mile Marathon Through
North America's Stolen Land*

ACCORDION EULOGIES

A MEMOIR OF MUSIC, MIGRATION, AND MEXICO

NOÉ ÁLVAREZ

CATAPULT  NEW YORK

ACCORDION EULOGIES

First Catapult edition: 2024

ISBN: 978-1-64622-089-2

Library of Congress Control Number: 2024930645

Jacket design and illustration by Nicole Caputo
Book design by Olenka Burgess

Catapult
New York, NY
books.catapult.co

Printed in the United States of America

10 9 8 7 6 5 4 3 2 1

La risa es el lenguaje del alma.

—PABLO NERUDA

Para mi Río. Nunca dejes de reír.

CONTENTS

VERSE

THE SEA INSIDE ME

I AM HOUNDED BY THE SPECTER OF A GRANDFATHER I NEVER REALLY knew. He was a migrant and a traveling musician, propelled by the songs that clamored in his chest. A man who gambled his lands away and left his wife and son to go hungry. After his disappearance, my grandmother died, leaving her young son—my father—homeless in Mexico.

My father was deeply bruised by this abandonment, this subjection to suffering at such a young age. It diminished his trust in others, calloused his heart, and made him in many ways more distant than the stars. My grandfather's absence echoed through the generations, altering my childhood as well as my father's. For years, my father has lived without closure. I've spent my life fruitlessly trying to close his hurt for him.

Because my grandfather was not present in our lives, I grew up unable to make him answer for the childhoods he denied us. I could never confront him for stripping my father of his ability to express love toward himself and his children in the way we needed. I yearned to tell my grandfather of the great man my father became in his absence, who migrated from Mexico to Yakima, Washington, stricken with fear, and made a family there; of the warrior I have become in the aftermath of my grandfather's mess, raised by the son my grandfather neglected. I longed to show him that what I am today stems entirely from my father's hard lessons and that nothing about the previous generation lives inside me.

But this would be a lie. Something of my grandfather is alive inside of me, I know, and it grows stronger every day—an inheritance of the accordion, dark shadows, and the impulse to be always on the move.

My grandfather held music more tightly than he held his children. In the stories that relatives tell about him, he drowned himself in fiestas and Mexican ballads, swept up in the sorrows and heroic battles narrated in corrido music.

I was raised on these Mexican ballads, lyrical accounts that have always offered me a medium for understanding the world of my ancestors. These songs have linked me to our people—people making music out of hard circumstances—like a vital artery. Now, through these corridos, I have decided to unearth my grandfather's story, to find him and secure his proper place in family folklore.

His name is Eulogio—or *eulogy*—an emblem of all the things we mourn in life. I will venture into learning music that can help me understand Eulogio's world and his decisions. I will hold an accordion between my hands and invoke its ancient gestures in order to peel back the layers of myself. Some of us grasp in our hands the things we cannot always keep hold of in our hearts. We stuff away the things we cannot yet come to terms with about ourselves: that no matter how hard we might try to escape, we are manifestations of our ancestral tragedies.

I am part of a long line of men who are lost at sea inside themselves. Men who have accumulated hurt but have long used their music to learn to move more lovingly in the world. I hope to do the same.

The day has come to account for the stories that failed me. To give them peace and let them go with music.

THE DREAMS ONLY CHILDREN CAN EXPERIENCE

(Yakima)

DECADES AGO, IN THE CRISP MORNING OF THE COUNTRYSIDE WHERE coyotes stalk the land, a mother swaddles her two babies in delicate fabrics and lays them to rest inside a wooden apple bin, hiding them in the heart of the orchard before she retreats into the apple trees to work. Only four walls shield her babies from the sword-swaths of the desert valley winds.

Their father keeps close watch from atop a diesel tractor, now and then forklifting his bin of babies through the land. He nuzzles them between trees and comforts them in his own secret way, blanketing them in a dialect before he falls back into the wild landscape. Every day, these parents surrender their babies to the spirits rustling in the sage. And every day the babies wait for their parents to reemerge from the canopy of trees, tired and weathered.

Out here, the babies live free of the fear that grips their

parents. They breathe the orchard essence, the wafting hints of sage and diesel, and absorb the traces of corrido music that convey to them the dreams their parents will never fully realize: the privilege of true liberation. This is a dream that will fall upon their shoulders. To this cursed land, the parents entrust their babies to survive.

For the duration of the workday, the parents retreat into the bush knowing that "los hijos son prestados"—that children are only borrowed. Passing spirits. Children belong to the spirit of the land and they will one day grow up and be summoned to put their bodies to it. They will be called away from home and away from the protection of their families. The parents take comfort in this sentiment—that the children are only borrowed—to keep from falling to pieces in a world filled with loss.

That we are transient beings is one of the many immigrant experiences that corrido music describes. It is a genre of accordion music that speaks of immigrant tragedies in the hopes that expressing pain might soften it. In the orchards, this accordion music resonated from radios, doing its best to ease the grueling days of picking fruit.

From these orchard bins my sister and I emerged, taking our first steps into a world of hard destinies. We peered over the edges of the boxes and watched the world of work that awaited us—a fate that had already been written in song. There in Yakima, hidden among tall blades of grass sharp enough to draw blood, we were immersed in our ancestral narratives.

Since birth, I have been shaped by the spirit of a people too well acquainted with hard landscapes. Corrido music came to me through the apple trees that held back the beating sun while farmer families hauled fruit using bags strapped to their bodies like accordions. Day after day, my parents filled their chests with the weight of their past, unable to put into words the trauma of two worlds: the violence of their Mexican homeland, and now their displacement into this English-speaking country that cast them into the shadows.

As a boy, I had heard accordions in Yakima that expressed their sound in warm and seedy places, the taverns and dance halls and house parties where tired migrants gathered to find relief. When the musicians played, I experienced a sound that felt as if it had been unleashed by spirits. The music gripped me by the throat and urged me to take bold action; to always carry the fire that my people held for one another.

Now, as an adult, I will teach myself to play the accordion. I will try to reenter the spiritual realms that corridos made present and real in my childhood. By taking up the instrument, I hope to speak the inherited sadness I have been unable to express for years.

When I strap the instrument to my body and put my heart against this power source, I will turn my mind to those two babies in the apple bin. The box is the shape that oppressed, comforted, defined, and ultimately saved me by protecting me from the harsh orchards. Now, I will hold the box of the accordion, reclaiming the shape as a site of power.

SOFTENING THE BLOWS

(Boston)

I SIT ALONE AGAINST AN APPLE TREE IN SUNDERLAND, MASSACHU-
setts, eating a kielbasa hot dog and waiting for a music store to
open. As I eat, I think about the improbable number of lives
my grandfather lived, the various jobs he held. But then I look
at myself and all my transformations, all the different jobs I've
held, and I realize that this is another way in which he and I are
alike. We are both easily dissatisfied, unable to sit with anything
for too long. Perhaps this restlessness is based in some shared dis-
trust of the world. We are each pulled toward constant change
because those other places always seem like they'll be better than
wherever we are, where the world seems to move too slowly. Too
oppressively. Perhaps, in all our exertions and self-reinventions,
we seek to keep the demons off our trails. Perhaps we cannot

come to terms with the finiteness of life and so we try to stretch it out by living on the move.

It's here in Sunderland that I begin my journey with the accordion, on the hunt for a model that's hard to find. At the Button Box music store, I will connect with a long line of artisans who have built accordions by hand since 1914—the Italian Castagnari accordion. I was introduced to the true profundity of the Castagnari sound from a video I'd found online, of the musician Patrícia Pereira playing the song "Djevoujka" on the streets of Lisbon. As I sit under the tree like a fallen apple, I rewatch the video on my phone.

Pereira begins the song slowly and I am immediately absorbed by the intensity of her gestures. She pulls at the bellows as if reeling in something deep and heavy from the Lisbon streets. Then, the pace of the music accelerates. Her fingers whip quickly through the notes, ensnaring me in her vision. Every time I watch the video, I am moved by the depth of her expressiveness and I long to feel things with that degree of conviction. My desire to pursue the accordion seriously starts with watching her. But she plays a higher-caliber triple-row accordion, which is unthinkable to me as a beginner. When the store opens, I will purchase a two-row instrument.

Inside, I browse the aisles, surrounded by an array of accordions. The used ones are lacquered and alive with the touch of their former owners. Generations of lessons are now within my reach, collecting dust in varied shapes and colors: ivory white, obsidian black, cigar-box browns, and cherry woods. Buttons dazzle in the light and piano keys resemble sinister smiles. Their fancy grilles remind me of luxury cars. Somewhere on these walls is the accordion that might help give me language to express myself.

Each specimen is an example of incredible craftsmanship. The process was developed nearly two centuries ago by the

Austrians, manufactured by the Italians, and transported to Latin America and the Caribbean by the Spaniards and the Germans. Part of why the accordion took off in many markets—including China, Ireland, Australia, and Africa—is because it was capable of adapting to the changing circumstances of many different communities.

When I finally see the accordion that's right for me, I take off my watch, removing the obstruction of time to fully inhabit this moment. I slip my arms into the close-fitting straps. They feel like restraints, as if they're meant to hold back whatever madman might arise within me when I play. When I arch my back to counterbalance the accordion's weight, my sternum pops into place.

I've long been haunted by feelings of darkness, unable to locate their source. But now I have a chance to hold that darkness between my hands, to give it form and language and to send it back into the world. What was once an invisible ailment has taken the shape of this instrument.

I know that the accordion will help me become something beautiful. But the sight of it is also bittersweet. It will always remind me that at the instrument's core are the struggles of my family's past.

And so, with a gesture to the relatives, I lay down money and devote myself to the Castagnari. I exit the shop with a seven-pound heart in my hands, ready to cut down demons.

EL MALIGNO

AS PART OF MY LEARNING, I BEGIN DELVING INTO THE FOLKLORE OF accordions. A story drifts to me from the shores of northern Colombia in La Guajira; a tale that beats strongly inside the indigenous heartland. It is the legend of "Francisco, El Hombre"—a villager who embodied the wayward ways of my migrant relatives. Long ago, this poor minstrel moved between dusty villages on a mule, the way my father did as a small boy in Mexico. Francisco played his accordion and took swigs from his rum gourd and lived inside a desert heat that maddened him with thoughts of death.

Though the landscape oppressed him, he also wanted to describe it through music, which gave him a language to express the inexpressible. That's the way of land: it robs the body of its strength but invigorates it with spirit. Francisco's accordion brought merriment to his people and protected them from evil forces. It squashed the darkness within him when he sang of love and death: "Este es el amor, amor/ El amor que me divierte / Cuando estoy en la parranda / No me acuerdo de la muerte."

Francisco spent many nights riding his donkey into the dark mountains alone, playing his accordion. As he played one day, the legend goes, a sinister echo resounded back at him from the misty woods. Spellbound, he followed the melody deep into the bush, into the wild realms beyond any human trespass, determined to find its source. He tried to pinpoint its location by playing a few measures of music and following the direction of the measures that played back to him.

As Francisco rallied back and forth with the echo, he noticed that the music coming back to him was changed. He realized that this sound was something more than just a playful fellow musician. It was cursed. It was el maligno. The devil's appearance was a sign that Francisco's talent had entered the realm of the impermissible, had cracked the natural order of things and aggravated the darkness. Fearing for his life, he played his accordion harder, trembling as he tried to keep back the demon that had now begun to swarm around him. But an even more powerful melody thundered back at him, too enchanting to escape.

When the mist cleared, revealing the moon's full glare, Francisco finally saw the demon before him, holding the most majestic accordion any man had ever seen. Demons, his people knew, were the original forgers of the accordion. They would pursue anyone who challenged their mastery of the instrument, the way Francisco had done without realizing. The cool wind had stiffened Francisco's fingers. He knew his life was ensnared in a battle with an enemy he could not run away from. He continued to duel with el maligno, their playing ratcheting up in intensity, until

Francisco emerged the winner. This legendary duel is also the origin story of vallenato, the famous Colombian rhythm of today.

These stories of music's spiritual power lure me in, pull me toward my own demonic battles with an elusive past. Through these sacred melodies, I hope to find a way to heal from the trauma of my family's history—the same way music bandaged my relatives, who poured their gritty experiences on farmlands into accordions.

━◆◆◆◆◆━

I was in my last days in my apartment in Boston, in a world of moving boxes and half-packed belongings, when I finally dared to pick up the instrument for the first time since I'd purchased it a few days back. I had chosen the imported Italian Castagnari solely for its links to the working man, though I also found its wooden design appealing. There it was, eager to breathe and speak through me; to share the countless tales of the demon who'd forged it and of all the souls imprisoned within it. I put my ear over my accordion case like a conch, as if to hear the distant echoes of all that my people dreamed.

I paced my apartment in some distress. I was anxious about the upcoming move back to Washington State, where my parents had once worked in the orchards. I tried to shake off the terrifying feeling that the move would not solve anything; that out there, beyond my door, there might still be nothing to bring me calm. I struggle with my sense of restlessness. In some ways, I see it as my family's curse—that our wandering is a way to avoid confronting things. We are a family that has kept our distance from our past and from one another, traveling far on foot and in spirit. We harden up our children with stories of the powerlessness and suffering we've endured so that they may do better than we did, and in doing so, we make them feel that they must run in order to avoid the same fate.

But our curse is not just our tendency to wander. Our curse is in our hardness, in our failure to express the soft things in our hearts to our children. The curse is in not knowing enough of our past and being content to live with the fragments. It is having to live in this state of irresolution, existing without the direction of our elders while also feeling responsible for their mistakes. The curse stems from my grandfather's choice to live in his own way, without his family and my father by his side.

I go for a walk, thinking about how I might remedy this breach. I think about the incomplete history that my grandfather left behind; how this absence spiritually impoverished my family and buried my grandfather's legacy in silence. With the aid of the accordion, I want to give new life to these spirits.

After I relocate to the Puget Sound region of Washington State, I decide I will travel to Mexico. The past may be in fragments, but this heart is still intact.

––––

In the days leading up to the move, I look out my apartment window and trace my reflection in the big Boston landscape and beyond, contemplating the tales I've heard of the elusive grandfather who moved in the shadows of Mexico. It's where he still lives, and where I briefly met him years ago. It is where I will journey to meet him again.

I grab hold of the accordion and release its treacherous breath, giving liberty to its sweet, sad sounds. With this act, I give myself over to the demon imprisoned inside of it—inside of me. I allow it to ensnare me on its journey, to take me by the hand and drag me from American town to Mexican village, the wild places of my people's stories. I have no other choice: If I shun the instrument and turn my back on the past, I will drown in my family's enduring tragedy. To lock the instrument back into its case would be to lock up my spirit.

My interest in the accordion is not just because it can unearth my family's stories. It is also a way to link me to a global network of accordionists who are doing similar work reclaiming their sound and reconnecting with their people. The accordion is the chosen instrument of many ethnic groups who suffered isolation and separation but still persevered. I will connect with these players as I learn to articulate my own story. I will travel to their homelands and immerse myself in their lives and in the gestures of their music, the accordion a visual symbol of our shared resistance.

My grandfather is one of these players too. The days are near when I will visit with this mystical man who used music to make sense of his migratory life. I hope to retrace his steps and revive the spirit of the accordion in our family. As I try to understand more of my grandfather's legacy, I also hope to learn the meaning of my own. He was a home-wrecker, a drunk, a gambler; a man forever caught in the currents of migration. Might the instrument have served and saved him, and could it play a similar role in my life? Or is my pursuit of the accordion just a desperate attempt to give love to something—and someone—who is unworthy of it?

TWO WINDS

GROWING UP, WHENEVER I HEARD ABOUT MY GRANDFATHER, HE WAS clouded in the mysteries of village folklore. Bits of him came to me by way of my distant elders—people who either loved or hated him. Whichever it was, family members were mostly wary of resurrecting his name. Instead, they corked his story into a bottle and tossed him to the torrential waters as flotsam for me to recover.

The village people say different things about him. That his soul wanders the old lands like a stray dog, in purgatory for the deeds of his past and for the families he has hurt. That he's a shape-shifting trickster living out his last days alone, anchored to nothing but scraps of old dreams, reliant on the kindness of others to sustain him. Of his playing, some say that this man had harnessed the powers of our people in his hands, that he mastered the sounds of the motherland in all its grief and glory. That his accordion held the rhythms that determined the outcome of village events and foretold the tragedies of the poor. Others say not *foretold*, but *inflicted*. But his music was also rumored to placate wild spirits, pull them into dance, give the villagers whatever peace could be had. Through his playing, he ushered people to their place of destiny, offering clarity on their journeys. The living danced along with the dead. Perhaps these were all lies and euphemisms to placate children. Still, this mythical power of his accordion—destructive or otherwise—intrigued and unsettled me.

Sometime in my twenties, years before I lived in Boston, I took an ancient route to visit Mexico. I was driven by dusty dreams and a handful of chicken buses, escorted by my maternal grandfather, who knew the area well. He was my protector inside a murderous, militarized, and illegally mined land that was perennially gripped by mafia warfare. In my back pocket I carried a journal with a treasure map to my origin story—sketches my father had made for me that outlined directions to a village by way of landmarks and rivers. Wedged between the pages of my journal was a picture of my paternal grandfather, strapped to a piano accordion that seemed to have a smile of its own.

Back then, I wasn't in Mexico to find my grandfather, just to learn the basics of my family history. Because no one could really tell me about my family's experiences, of the songs that had once coursed through us but got buried in the trauma of harvesting harsh landscapes, I made it my mission to pursue the story of my ancestors from Michoacán. I longed to know how our stories got displaced through migration, discarded on the journey to El Norte—which included the story of my grandfather, the traveling musician.

On that trip, while I was visiting a beach, my paternal grandfather appeared to me in the flesh, having tracked the scent of distant kin. Somehow, word must have reached him that I was visiting. He was a thin wire of a man in a loosely buttoned shirt, slacks, and dress shoes made dusty by many pilgrimages. He approached me against the backdrop of a violent ocean, its waves chomping the shore like sharks' teeth.

This man came to me like a sudden mist from somewhere over the mountains. He had emerged from the no-man's-land of Tierra Caliente, Michoacán, determined to see the shape of me and, perhaps, to try to glimpse his own son within me. It's possible he wanted to witness the lives he had abandoned ages ago, and to reconcile through me what he couldn't do with my father or with his music: to restore the sacred link to our family.

My grandfather walked toward me with steps that barely seemed to make an imprint in the sand. His eyes were fixed on something far away. Here we were, two strange specimens from different worlds, like two winds colliding to make a tornado. Wordlessly, he removed something from his back pocket—a glass Coca-Cola bottle he had filled with homegrown tobacco. He squatted under a palm tree that faced the ravenous ocean. From his shirt pocket he pulled a corn husk that he rolled into a cigarette. I sat on the sand next to him. The Pacific Ocean's treacherous waters clawed at our feet.

"So, you're Huicho's son?" His exhale was smoky. Huicho is my father's nickname.

I answered yes, my eyes too caught up with tracing his shape before it eroded away into the sand.

We talked into the night, drawing out our stories as hungrily as the frenzied mosquitoes drew out our ancient blood.

Years ago, when I'd visited Mexico as a child, I could not understand what I'd missed by not having a relationship with my grandfather. It was only here, in this brief encounter, that I realized how big the void inside me was from having grown up without him. I knew the past was painful; that he'd allowed destruction to come my father's way and that destruction then blew into my own life. But at that moment I felt only warmth for him and for how free he seemed to be, how content and at peace. As I watched him squatting under a tree, curious and childlike about the world, I finally observed a bit of myself in him. I felt myself in his soft gaze that settled onto things with feather-like gentleness, searching for the teachable moments in everything he saw. Now, those eyes swept over mine as he slicked his side hairs upward with his fingers, giving him the wispy look of a wolverine.

During this short meeting, we became quick friends, two schemers committed to exploration. Our time together was filled with strange conversations and the small gifts of his storytelling. I still remember him leaning in to ask: "Is it true what they say?"

"What's that?"

"That the world is round?"

For him, wandering was a form of protest. He loved to camp outdoors or as close to it as possible, living the irrational life of a dreamer in an isolated landscape. I spent that evening in his home, a cinder-block shack with only three walls and a tin roof—a horse stable, really.

The evening was thick with stars and geckos and with the desert ghosts of the Tierra Caliente region—traces of people who had been taken violently from this land. My grandfather lit a candle and leaned back onto his hammock. Lying under the night sky, he rolled himself another smoke and sat suspended in thought, meditating over every drag as if every breath meant something sacred to him.

I knew that he had migrated plenty, had built many stories and family clusters in Mexico and the United States. It bothered me that he had never passed down any of his teachings to my father, or to me; that he had kept the special magic of our land and our origin story to himself. But perhaps this wisdom was earned, not given. Perhaps he was still feeling me out, still suspicious of my spirit. So I did not ask.

He told me to set my bag down and to step aside while he perused a heap of junk in a dark corner—an alchemist's workshop of dismantled metal, electronics, and papers. Some of it, he said, were his investigations into the Spanish treasure in the area—a hunt that got curtailed by the mafias sprouting up around him. But the people were rising up, he assured me, and soon he'd be on his way back to his gold.

"Ah, here it is," he said. From the rubble, he pulled out a metal detector. He squinted and prodded at its buttons before handing it to me. "I haven't been able to make it work. But if you want, we can go try it out someday."

He continued rummaging through the pile. I saw no sign of the accordion I had seen in pictures of him. I wondered if he had traded it away or had it dismantled and repurposed. Once he found what he'd been looking for, he traced the walls with a homemade pesticide that burned my sinuses. The concoction was not for the tarantulas, cockroaches, or snakes that were so common in the area, but for the scorpions clustered inside the walls.

At that point in the visit, older memories started coming back to me, of past visits to Mexico when I was younger. I remembered wandering my grandfather's land barefoot, on the hunt for plums, until a scorpion jammed its stinger into my fleshy foot and summoned me into a feverish dream. I spent some weeks in a damp slumber, at the mercy of the poison coursing through me. In this devil's dream I was also with my grandfather, an indigenous man in manta (wild cotton used in traditional Mexican clothing), a straw hat, and sandals. I was swaying on his hammock next to him and his accordion. I was swallowed whole by the music that he played, dazed with wonder at this instrument and what it meant to wandering men of the mountains like my grandfather.

Wondering what it could mean to me in my hands.

"This will be your bed," he told me now. The cot was low to the ground and constructed by hand, crosshatched with thread in the indigenous tradition that would leave me with a checkered back in the morning. There was no mattress. It was just short of sleeping on a mound of straw. A cowboy's nest.

On that visit, just as quickly as my grandfather appeared in my life, he vanished. While I was visiting other relatives the next day, he called me and urged me to leave town immediately. Some people had come to his house to inquire about me and who I was. Bad people in armored Escalades who were looking to interrogate me about my business.

"Leave your things here," he said distantly over the phone. "I'll take care of them. Just don't come back."

That was all I heard before the connection was cut. His name, his story retreated from me once again. These harsh lands sent me running from my story, from any chance of reconciling the past with the fragile present. Instead, they uprooted me and launched me back to where I came from.

I think of all the ways my people run—of the migratory patterns that mark us and the stories that we tell about our wounds in song. Corridos are passed down orally, inherited from prior generations. Since their inception, they have served as a form of musical newspaper. Their lyrics might tell stories of oppression, or poetic renderings of daily life, or tales of criminality. The ballads have a long history that dates back to before the Mexican War, when they detailed the struggles of farmers, the clashes of Prohibition-era tequileros (smugglers), and political uprisings.

The origin of the word *corrido* means "to run." To run with your story and carry it over vast landscapes. This act of preservation is a way of life. For many people, it is the only way to document the harsh circumstances they endure—as Mexican campesinos (farm workers), soldiers, or smugglers, for example. Corridos are what villagers use to build a record, often in the face of violent and inevitable displacements that force the life of migrants upon us.

Since I was a child in the orchards, I inherited the mentality embodied by corridos: to be always on guard, vigilant, ready to run at a moment's notice. This awareness runs thick in my Mexican blood. Mine is a heritage steeped in corrido narratives, a difficult history full of death that reminds me we are a persecuted people still.

For years, I ran in order to find myself. I ran from the corrido narratives that chased me in my youth. I ran from the tales that haunted my family and sought to bind me to a past I did not always want to confront. I knew that to look directly at the corridos—at the stories of my family—would reveal too much pain.

Only now, when my grandfather is in frail condition in an obscure village, am I ready to look more closely. I am determined to pick up where he and I left off years ago, to infiltrate his lands again before the ancestors take him away for good. I will unlock the stories trapped in his music and stir up old ghosts in a land at war with itself.

UN PUÑO DE TIERRA

AS A CHILD IN THE ORCHARDS OF YAKIMA, WHEN SPIRITS HUNG LOW like morning fog, I listened to the echoes of my people working deep inside the fields. When I could no longer hear the trees rustling with laborious picking, I would find my way back to my parents from the faint sounds of their radio. These radios were perched under picking ladders, playing música norteña, rancheras, banda, mariachi, cumbia: the sound of trembling accordions that captured our story as a migrant family. My parents wailed along to this music, which gave them space to cry inside the canopy of fruit trees.

I wandered the orchards under the spell of corridistas—musicians whose spitfire fingers flew over their three-row accordion keys. Música norteña—a genre that originated in northern

Mexico—gave voice to the disempowered men and women of Yakima who lived and labored apart from their motherland. Music ameliorated things for them, preserved their connection to their culture, especially when they could not always express it. People like my parents could not always openly exhibit their pain to their children, who were still too fragile to know the truth of this land. But I knew. I felt it in the vividness of their work, the intensity of their sweat, and the cries of the accordion.

There's a corrido song by the Mexican artist Ramón Ayala, known as the "King of the Accordion," called "Un Puño de Tierra" (A Fistful of Dirt). It explains the migrant condition well, narrating the way our life is defined by movement. The song is about a man who travels from port to port, living out an existence that's always too brief and never allows him to put down roots. All we have are memories, Ayala sings, and in the end, all that we will take to the grave is a fistful of dirt. "Un Puño de Tierra" is part of a tradition of songs that aim to ground us in the very dirt that migrants harvest. It keeps us stable in an unstable world while also reminding us of our inevitable journey back into the soil.

Corrido music helped us celebrate the small things. It resounded in the migrant camps of the Yakima Valley, in the crowded households of my relatives, and over carne asadas where people danced through the spaces that lay claim to them, trying to stamp out their pain, if only for an evening. This was the music that formed my worldview and ways.

From the beginning, adults told me to know my story well. They told me that I could carry myself out of the tragedy of place and conquer any landscape so long as I made the time and space to speak my pain. But even though I lived within and alongside this sad music, as a boy, I could not always digest it. I did not always want to feel the sadness of my people.

Music connects us with the narratives of our forebears. Through instruments, we are able to give voice to our ancestors while also pushing out our own sound into existence. I look to the previous generations as metronomes that mark the passage of time, and I trace the songs that I play back through a long lineage of travelers, musicians, and storytellers. It is important to know the history, because the musical knowledge of our elders is also fading. Though the accordion still thrives in many parts of the world, it is disappearing in the United States.

I study the accordion's expansive reach across the globe. A world away, villages are under the spell of the bayan accordion. Elsewhere, Cajun and Creole ballads resound from single-row accordions in the bayous of Louisiana. Everywhere, it seems, there is an accordionist who softens the blows of life with music.

In a video from Argentina, there might be a gaucho slumbering in the grassy Pampas, where winds make waves of the horizon. His instrument is the bandoneon accordion, which originated in Germany and was imported into Argentina by European immigrants. This gaucho sits by the campfire, packing yerba into his mouth like tobacco chew. When he plays, his music is alive with the sounds of its African heritage, which gave birth to the tango.

After watching a number of these scenes, I unlock my accordion case and prepare to invoke my place among my own ancestral ghosts. Perhaps I will even connect with my grandfather. I place my fingers onto the keys. Through my music, I am transported into a different world.

Suddenly I am among the Pampas with a gourd of mate beside me, sitting by a campfire. I am among ancestors. I continue to lay down my musical notes, casting my energy into their fire, until I finally feel ready to speak. I hear myself hurl the first words at my grandfather, who sits next to me in this circle of elders: "What about us hurts you, abuelo? What embers burn you so much that you never look back at the trail of hurt you left?"

There are so many dark spaces left in our narrative by people who left and never looked back. I too left my hometown of Yakima and have only just begun to look back at the destruction caused by my departure; at the relationships I failed to build, the funerals I failed to attend. But unlike my grandfather, my heart was always with my people.

The light of the campfire brings out his face and I keep pressing him for answers. "Was an accordion easier to bear than your family?"

In this dream he moves, extends his hand over the fire, and grasps at a colony of ash moths. He catches an ember and swallows it and all the light dies out, he and the elders dispersing with it into the Pampas. I pursue them and call out after him. But the only response is the sound of the wind slithering in the grass.

Perhaps my grandfather shuns me for the lack of skill in my playing. I still struggle over the sounds of my accordion and cannot yet make good music, cannot yet express the language that will capture his attention. My offering to him isn't good enough yet. I have still to earn my place in this story.

━━━━

After hours of accordion practice in my Boston apartment, watching videos and mimicking the movements of these other musicians, I lock the instrument back into its case. With the impatience of a tiger, I claw at clothing to dress myself for the day. I tear myself from my apartment and emerge into the big Boston landscape, taking the accordion with me.

I sit on a rock along the bank of the sleek Charles River. Nearby, a duck slurps up the algae around a bed of lily pads. It continues eating until the vegetation is parted by a team of Ivy League rowers who slash and skin the water with their oars. A woodpecker spirals up a tree while I rest my head on my hand. I scratch my scalp over the water's surface and feed the fish with flakes of dandruff.

In the end, all I am is fish food.

I continue to acquaint myself with my accordion. I replace the cacophony of city traffic with its sounds. A bee hovers nearby, touch-and-going over the lily pads, until a small fish launches into the sky and swallows it.

I sit here, ready to step again into the life of a traveler, a wanderer, a descendant of migrants with music as my passport. Soon, I will follow the sounds of the accordion to the American South, the first place I have decided to pursue the instrument's history. In Louisiana, I hope to trace many of the links that make up the accordion's history. Doing so might possibly help me understand my own.

JEFFERY BROUSSARD AND THE CREOLE COWBOYS

"They only give you flowers when you're dead"

I HAVE ARRIVED IN LOUISIANA—THE CULTURAL TERRAIN THAT HAS absorbed the stories of many displaced generations, including those of German, Creole, Irish, French, French Canadian, Native American, Anglo-American, Italian, and Spanish ancestry. Here, I will honor a tradition of Black Creole elders, tracing the legacy of musicians who inspired a wide range of Southern artists, including the Tex-Mex conjunto legend Flaco Jiménez. Jiménez's corridos were well known to migrants in Yakima. He once played alongside Clifton Chenier—the King of Zydeco, a genre that emerged from southwest Louisiana.

The accordion has had a fraught history in this region. When the oil industry boomed in Texas in the early twentieth century, it rapidly changed the way of life for the Black Creole and Cajun populations. Oil and rig-building brought jobs, highways were built to connect the once-isolated prairies to the outside world, agriculture became mechanized, and money filled pockets fast, elevating people's economic status.

But these innovations also destroyed some of the culture. Newly invented jukeboxes filled the dance halls and displaced the accordions, severing one connection to people's ancestral influences. School systems became homogenized and students were barred from learning or speaking the French language. Assimilation became the leading principle, and Cajuns and Creoles were discriminated against as a result.

The music became more commercialized too, with some artists forced to adopt English over French and to drop the accordion altogether. But by the 1960s, the people began to advocate for their traditions again. Artisans restored the one-row accordion that made the Creole sound distinctive. There was a resurgence in Cajun pride and embracing one's connection to the community's working-class roots. The language began to thrive again, with music helping to facilitate this cultural preservation.

The American South influenced the music that eventually made its way to Yakima. As a child in that community, I sometimes moved among the waves of Baptist bluegrass, under the wailing spirits of my surrogate grandparents, Bob and Claudette. They were farmers from another era who took my family in, steeping us in the ways of southern food, gospel, and bare-bones kindness while I was still learning English.

I recall the small church on the outskirts of town in Naches, Washington, where dust plumes occasionally veiled it from view. It was a holy place that came and went like a passing rain, summoning a sandstorm of elders who knew of old times and children who were eager to learn them. The people gathered there in dusty boots, cowboy hats, and suspenders. During sermons, the banjos and accordions seemed to duel with demons. The spirit struck the congregants like lightning; as a child, I feared being struck too, thrust into an experience I might not be able to handle. But as I watched the bodies drop around me, I saw them lifted up again by folk music and accordions, which seemed to carry a healing power.

To the congregants, the songs painted vivid pictures of home, the lands of Montana and Oklahoma they still yearned for. I never forgot the fervor of this place and this community, the coatings of dust on their faces. Because of the musical vibrancy of the American South, I sometimes even felt enthusiasm for this oppressive land. At times, I even forgot about the legacies of violence permeating our landscapes. The musical tradition Bob and Claudette introduced me to is one thing I hope to rediscover in Louisiana.

There is one man in particular I want to meet. Down south in old Opelousas lives a bruised man with a story to tell, a zydeco legend: Jeffery Broussard of the Creole Cowboys. On my first day in Louisiana, I step into the back seat of his Land Rover in Lafayette. He and his wife Millie had insisted on picking me up.

"It's the way we do things down here," Millie says, putting out her last cigarette. After we embrace, we drive into their cicada-buzzing homeland. All around me, I hear the sounds of French Creole.

"You're with family now, brother," Jeffery says. His voice carries grit, calloused and worn down by many hard years living as a Black man in southwest Louisiana. He sings just to be heard, he tells me, "just trying to make a living."

We slip through an endless landscape of haggard moss that clings to old oaks and dilapidated structures. The land is quiet, as if in mourning. Hard histories permeate everything, including Jeffery's words. He is a respected elder now, but he lived a reckless life in his younger days. He has dedicated years to rebuilding his life by way of playing the accordion. Today, he helps many folk heal through zydeco traditions, sharing music that is firmly grounded in their hard histories.

"It's music that holds a lot of sadness," he says. It can be "about a child who died or went to prison, or someone who worked hard all his life" for low pay, or someone's mule. It is music that also finds comedy in tragedy, tackling themes that are relatable to the local populations.

But the landscape of zydeco is also changing, and Jeffery is fighting to preserve the tradition. "Today's kids don't wanna hear [about] that. They wanna hear about the fast life. The fast money."

For nearly two decades, Jeffery played with a group called Zydeco Force—a nouveau zydeco group in the 1980s that he describes as one of the "three hottest groups" of the genre at the time and pioneers in introducing harmony. He was part of the same scene as the best of the Black Creole zydeco legends, like Stanley "Buckwheat" Dural and Clifton Chenier. He learned his craft by living the life of zydeco: he started his life picking potatoes for money and later turned to the accordion as a way to survive and to provide for his family. He is a man who can play, talk, sing, and smoke, all with a cigarette and a toothpick in his mouth, at the same time. "Nothing can break my concentration," he tells me. Or his will to survive.

In the landscape, signs of life die down as we drive over large expanses of prairie land. "It makes me feel good to help people," Jeffery says. "That part of me will live on in the music that I pass down to others. I'm about saving our music. Singing about the life that we live." As he sees it, zydeco embodies the ups and downs of the Black man's experience: the racist encounters on the streets like when he dated a "some-timing white girl" (who was sometimes racist and sometimes not) and the white folk who tried running him down in a car for dating her in public. "They ran over my fiddle but not my bones," he says, laughing. "I had to fight a lot growing up. To stay alive."

After a long trip through this southern dreamscape, we come upon ranchlands deep in the prairies of Prairie Ronde. Here, where life stands still, Jeffery and Millie compose music and live out their years in peace.

I step into the misty haze of this ancient, humid earth. Swarms of swallows cluster inside a canopy of oaks. Horses whip mosquitoes with their tails; roosters clear their throats and call out like the cholos who used to rough me up in Yakima. Standing on the lawn, I feel some sadness—it is a garden of remembrance where statues of angels and cowboys kneel before the crosses of loved ones. While Jeffery and Millie gather themselves, I rest for a moment on an outdoor rocking chair that moves me between the past and the present, swaying me between what was and what is still to come, stewing in this dream that is Louisiana.

Inside, their home is bright with color and affirmations like CHERISH LIFE, EMBRACE YOUR DREAMS, BELIEVE IN YOUR HEART. A chandelier is suspended above a dinner table covered in dripping candles. They notice me looking at some purple flowers in a copper vase in their kitchen.

"Here in these parts, they only give you flowers when you're dead," Jeffery says, referring to the handful of local artists who weren't acknowledged when they were alive. His song "I Wonder Why" speaks to that reality.

Looking through the kitchen window, I see an oxidation pond in the backyard and a shed where their son lives. I realize that the pond—wastewater—is alive with something. The groaning and growling sounds like a hog, but the sounds are coming from a gator. The Broussards live with a creature that has made his kingdom in the wastewater. The animal shadows Jeffery like the demons he carries.

"We like him there," he says.

◆◆◆◆

When the night thickens, we move to the back of the house, to a room sectioned off in the back of Jeffery's garage. I stop at the threshold, sensing a powerful energy that almost calls for smudging. This is much more than a music studio. I split the lacy curtains and step into the embryo of all that is Jeffery and all that is zydeco. Here is where Jeffery gives everything to his work and where his heart and soul are unmade and remade daily in music. It is where he gathers with the ghosts of his past in Creole ceremony.

"It's not zydeco when you get away from your roots," he explains. "Zydeco is not just having an accordion, it's not just a moneymaker. It's not a commercial thing. It is the recognition of our elders. It is respect dedicated to them."

The origin of the word *zydeco* is said to stem from the French Creole colloquial expression for "poverty" or "times are tough" (les haricots sont pas salés, or "the snap beans are not salty"). Jeffery tells me that zydeco is a "snappy beat," like the snap beans.

"They're good only if you prepare them correctly and if you add some salt, some soul, some heart."

The music was popularized in the 1960s by the King of Zydeco, Clifton Chenier, who learned the basics of accordion under his father's tutelage. He moved between jobs cutting sugarcane in the fields of New Iberia, Louisiana, to hauling oil trucks in Texas, where he played accordion at the gates of the dirty refineries. Chenier first found inspiration in the ancient sound of juré—a form of a cappella call-and-response that contains clapping and stomping. He began to incorporate more aspects of his Creole heritage into the music and eventually became a leading force in helping to spread it globally.

On the walls of Jeffery's music room are images of Christ and the Virgin Mary, the words "Mon Seul Espoir" and "Marie Reine De La Paix," and a number of photographs. Through the pictures, I trace his life journey. The images offer insight into who he really is, as well as what he guards from the public. Around the room's array of keyboards, electric guitars, and fine accordions, the walls are also cluttered with accolades, posters, newspaper clips, and images of Jeffery in his cowboy hat and attire. They carry his wounds too, including one particular sore spot—a black-and-white photo of a man strapped to an accordion on a lonesome prairie. A brother who died in a house fire. There's also a framed picture of a bandmate that Jeffery lost to drugs, and of his father and family members who lived their own struggles.

They are here with him always.

"I should have been dead," he says, as he tells me about the many times he could have lost his life by living recklessly. It is in this spirit that he rededicates himself to the ceremony of zydeco. "Zydeco is the bigger picture," he says. "It's when you give your whole heart to it.

"I go through a lot of pain," he tells me after a long silence, breaking down in tears. "My younger daughter is in and out of my life. My other child is in and out of trouble and my heart bleeds for my oldest son who is in and out of jail and battling with drugs." His eldest is currently incarcerated and faces life in prison. "A lot of my family are going about life the wrong way." He wipes his eyes. "But no matter how much my heart bleeds, I want to keep looking forward. I gotta stay strong. I've given my son back to God."

The rains begin to pelt the roof of the garage. I study the

grain of his accordions, how the wood around the area where his thumb goes is worn down by years of his grip; years of staying in the fight. The colors of the instruments are faded, stained by sweat so heavy it sometimes destroys the bellows.

I find hope in the spiritual experience of zydeco as he describes it. Zydeco narrates the hard times, yes, but also strives to liberate its listeners through song, dance, and forging connection with one's community. It encourages the listener to partake in the sacred ritual of shaking off one's trauma on the dance floor. An alternative translation of zydeco is "to dance," which evokes the social rituals of Black Creole communities. Zydeco dancing was a social event that affirmed community ties, rejecting white colonialism and helping the dancers escape their harsh circumstances, if only for a night. These dance halls helped revive the Black Creole movement when it was under threat from the pressure to assimilate. They also honored Creole contributions to the accordion.

I worry about carrying Jeffery's heavy stories properly in my writing, in my music. I lose sleep over telling them right. But he and I are also helping one another to find the medicine in our respective stories. There is power in verbalizing the pain, in listening and empathizing with the struggles of others.

◆◆◆◆

In the morning, before driving out into Creole country, Jeffery runs his hand inside the bed of his pickup truck over an area that had been charred by fire. A distressed family member stricken by drugs had set fire to his truck, near gas tanks that could have taken out the whole neighborhood. These are the realities that drive Jeffery's hard-hitting accordion style.

We jump into this truck and press into a world of prairies and bayous and pain, listening to Jeffery's heart-wrenching gospel mixes—the music of funerals, he calls it. He takes me to the town of Frilot Cove, where we drive along his childhood horseback trails. The roads are bumpy with potholes the size of snap turtles, creatures that sometimes reside here after storms. The truck bucks like a horse on what is now called "Raiders Road." Here, his people labored on hands and knees picking potatoes and pulling long, sharp grass-blades to clear the fields. Tough fields cut new landscapes into their palms. Now, only cows lie here, shouldering flocks of white cranes that sift through cow dung for sustenance.

"We were done with living in the country," Jeffery says of the sharecroppers who lived here under the rule of white landowners. "It was super hard living in the country, from 5:00 a.m. to 5:00 p.m." He recalls his time as a "potato boy," pointing to field after field of cotton and potato. "On our knees all day in those fields. Twenty, thirty of us out there on our knees."

In the time of slavery, most Black Creoles lived a miserable existence as field hands. Slave owners treated them as expendable and kept bringing in more labor from Africa and Haiti. The Black population in the South was in constant flux, and their music became infused with the strains of African and Haitian song, and was as well the vehicle for expressing the harsh realities of slavery. Before the accordion was introduced, people preserved this painful history in juré—the call-and-response songs with rhythms made by stamping, clapping, and shouting. They made music with their beaten bodies, never relinquishing the sounds of their homelands.

In time, the music evolved in tandem with the growing population of Cajuns—an American corruption of the French ethnic word *Acadien*—a people twice exiled, from France and from Nova Scotia. Cajuns settled Louisiana to become cattle ranchers, picking up the arts of the cowboy from Mexicans and Native Americans who were already living in the prairies. By the

1760s, these settlers were moving herds through swamps about one hundred years before the Texas trail rides began, using the skills of their French ancestors to adapt to their environment.

We pull up to a boyhood bayou of Jeffery's and stop on a nameless dirt road to look out from an overpass onto murky water that serpentines deep into the bush. It is a dump site for kitchen sinks, refrigerators, and chairs. A body of water choked off by rusted junk. Barbed wire runs up and down its banks.

"We used to go in there with pitchforks as boys, to hand-fish." Waist-deep in muddy water, Jeffery and his friends would stick their hands into holes for catfish to bring home to their families. If they wrapped their hands around a snake they'd yell "tide-eye" and scramble, or toss it to one another. "You were safer in the water than on the banks where snakes and gators rest," he says. They were careful not to draw blood for the alligators, the way his cousin once did when he stepped on razor-sharp scrap metal hidden in the murky water.

People throw their tires or old gas tanks into the water, leave them overnight, and come back to retrieve the fish that took shelter inside the junk—they call it "gas-tank fishing."

"See over there, where that refrigerator is, I bet you there's tons of big fish inside of it right now." Among the junk are larger items that got turned over by storms, like cars, that have become perfect fishing traps for poor locals.

We follow the bayous until they bring us to a house—the house owned by the person Jeffery's father worked for, who oversaw the labor of Black slaves.

"I seen my mom work too hard, picking cotton, potatoes. I promised myself never again." He tells me about his father, whom he'd carried a grudge about for a long time. "I would always hear how he was a family man, always a provider to other families. But growing up, I saw other things. Another side of him. He was a woman's man." One day, Jeffery raised the subject with his father when the two of them were out on a trail ride. To his surprise, talking about it brought them closer. "Dad would walk along these ditches with us—ditches that often flooded the streets and that we had to swim through with our bikes in tow to get back home." His father would carry a pitchfork and poke around, listening for the sound of metal against shell that alerted them to a snap turtle's presence. From his father, Jeffery learned to study the sounds of his environment. Sounds that often meant survival.

He points out other dilapidated farmhouses on all this sharecropper land—the places he and his community gathered over boucheries. "We were always at someone's house every week. We killed a pig and celebrated the time we had together."

These boucheries were core to zydeco's development. In earlier decades, the Creole communities who labored in the fields together would gather at harvest time for a family's bouchere ("butchering of a hog") to cook and share fresh meat. After the heavy fieldwork, the people would celebrate and entertain themselves with a La La, the French Creole term for "house dance." La Las were thrown outside of harvest season too. When times got tough for a family, communities might host a dance in someone's living room. They emptied out the furniture and would charge an admission fee and sell gumbo, homemade beer, and lemonade to raise funds for families in need.

"Nowadays you don't see this anymore," Jeffery says. "Things just changed." He lowers his eyes. "Families aren't as close as they used to be."

As well as house dances, La La was frequently played in rural dance halls and at social events in places like Opelousas and Marksville, and in east Texas near the border. The form was popularized by southwest Louisiana artists like Amédé Ardoin, who was born in Basile. Amédé would carry his accordion everywhere in a flour sack, as if his music were bread to feed the masses. His highly syncopated accordion style and improvisational lyrics were often inspired by the personal lives of the dancers in front of him. He was renowned for the emotion of his high, wailing voice and his impassioned playing.

He loved to compose songs about people working in the hot sun, who lived in the middle space of the hazy heat waves over the horizon. I am reminded of the migrants collapsing under the sweltering sun in Yakima to pick cherries in triple-digit weather.

The life of a working musician also moved Amédé into dangerous places, like white territories and dances. His was a very racially divided society, where Black men who entered those spaces ran a risk. Amédé's challenges to segregationist codes were legendary. Many times, he was run off by white men, taking off across fields and leaving his accordion nestled in the harvest. He would later recover it under cover of darkness.

"The white men wanted his music and not his face," Jeffery says. In Amédé's day, he was required to play at white events through a window wearing white gloves. Today, Jeffery finds that a lot of his audience is still white.

The next place Jeffery takes me is his mother's grave in Frilot Cove. He used to ride his horse to get here, a creature he named "B-Flat" and taught to prostrate before the ancient oaks. B-Flat carried him through his worst. He thought he had broken the horse, but in reality, the horse broke him.

"After gigs I'd get to missing my family and I'd get drunk and get onto my horse bareback at 2:00 or 3:00 a.m." Jeffery would ride B-Flat hard, straight to his mother's grave to talk with her. The horse knew the way.

"I was going through some things and I would ride and ride, talking with my horse. He was my guardian." Sometimes Jeffery would collapse over his horse, who'd carry him to the front steps of his house and wait until he dismounted.

We walk together onto the spongy earth near his mother's

grave. I tread carefully over the graveyard. Jeffery has come here with an accordion many times to play for his mother.

In any context, playing is a deeply emotional experience for him. He has to be careful of what will arise when he picks up the instrument. It brings up so much pain that he can feel powerless against it. Sometimes he has to go months without playing. "If I played accordion every day, I would lose my mind. I'd be full of hurt." He tears up again. "I play zydeco with a smile, meanwhile my heart is bleeding. You pretend to the public that everything is fine. A person never knows what you're going through."

Back in the car, we come to an area where trail rides grew to their biggest in the 1880s, during Creole country parties. Their roots date back to the 1760s, when French-speaking slaves from Africa started their own rodeos because they were banned from white-only events. In a nearby field is the historic Triangle Club—an old structure, long shuttered and sinking into a sea of tall grass, that once housed big names like Otis Redding, James Brown, Tyrone Davis, and Jeffery's father.

"See those two doors?" Jeffery points. "One entry was for the mulattoes, as they were called back then, the other side was for the Black folk." Many people in the community wanted to preserve their lightness and prohibited integration. "If you were too Black, others didn't want to associate with you. I remember back in the day, before entering the club, you first had to toss your hat in. If they tossed it back, you better not go in there."

His wife, Millie, would later tell me of the haircombs that people nailed at the threshold of their houses. "If your hair couldn't pass through without getting caught, you'd better turn yourself around." In other words, you were too Black and therefore unwelcome.

This was the double-edged reality that people, and zydeco, operated in until very recently. There were separate doorways and separate musical histories. The genre addressed these tensions head on: zydeco songs named the racial and economic tensions and stirred up calls for action and change. Spaces like the Triangle Club were also an opportunity to mix musical traditions, promoting an exchange of ideas between the white and Black working classes. Gathering in dance halls produced not only a cross-fertilization of Creole and Cajun music but also political causes, encouraging immigrants to unite around their shared experiences.

We stop to pick up Jeffery's brother Jerald and delve deeper into the grasslands and bayous, moving from one shuttered club to another, including Slim's Y-Ki-Ki, the Gin-Side Inn, Richard's Club, Papa Paul's, and the Wagon. I'm hotboxed in cigarette smoke and blasting zydeco music as the sun begins to set and thunderclouds start to collect on the horizon. We are cruising free under soft rain, hightailing it on roads the way I did in high school.

"Too many people got greedy and started too many clubs and dispersed the people," Jeffery suggests. "Back in the day, music veterans like Clifton Chenier showed up at clubs in support of one another. 'We're all gonna share the stage,' he'd say. We all win. It was a communal thing. Now, it's a dog-eat-dog world."

◆◆◆◆◆

That night, Jeffery has a zydeco show in Lafayette. While he prepares his gear, I stand outside with Jerald, who plays scrubboard in his brother's band. Jerald is a man who rarely speaks, preferring to stare into space and let his mind flow with the spirit of the land. He and I lean against cars in Jeffery's driveway, watching the sunset. Louisiana rewards people who know when to appreciate the silence, how to take in the land and absorb its teachings. The clouds crackle like knuckles in preparation for rain.

Jeffery finally comes out in his cowboy boots and getup, and we pack into a van with Jeffery's bandmates and their wives.

On the drive over, Jeffery tells us that he once turned down a chance to play with Tex-Mex legend Flaco Jiménez. "Hohner wanted us to play together, but with Hohner accordions." At the time, Hohner's reeds couldn't support Jeffery's hard-hitting style, so he turned down the sponsorship. "Also, bellows used to be made of cardboard back then and I used to sweat through them and break them."

After a short drive, the car pulls up at the club. Led Zeppelin's "Tangerine" is playing as we step into the soft bistro lighting at the Blue Moon Saloon. Here, Jeffery is welcomed by more of his crew, who are setting up their equipment on stage.

Jeffery has dressed for the occasion: he is wearing a baseball cap that says GOD, a flannel button-up shirt and jeans, a bedazzled belt buckle, and gator boots. His shirt buttons gleam against the stage lighting. One by one, he unlocks his accordions from their cases, airing them out in preparation for the damage they are about to do, the tussle they are about to have with the spirits of the crowd.

Here, Jeffery will engage in the age-old ceremony of zydeco, liberating us for a night from the harms of our own thoughts and ways. The band warms up. The drummer stomps the pedal, shaking my heart as if threatening to dislodge it from my chest. While storm clouds gather closer, the amplifiers thunder with electric guitar. The volume briefly robs me of my hearing, perhaps so that I may truly begin to hear again.

Jeffery slips his fingers over a single-row accordion, entering into a handshake with his ancestors. He wrings out the bellows of various two- and three-row instruments, pulling the air from them, forcing them to dislodge their secret magic. They resist, but he tames them like he has all his horses. He battles with the grand snakes of the bellows as if he were still a boy handfishing for sustenance in the bayous.

From the door, the famous accordionist and leading Creole fiddler Cedric Watson walks in with his wife. They have both come to support Jeffery. The two of them go way back, Cedric says. They used to ride horses together.

"I'm here to dance," he says before he starts to two-step under Jeffery's spell. When the show begins, more boots gather on the dance floor. The earth trembles.

Jeffery gets into motion, entering a sort of ecstasy, and dips his left hand as if to pour out the heavy contents of his accordion's bass side. His songs work on the nerves at all levels, moving into different depths of the listener's skin. The music works the knots out of the crowd's tight muscles. He moves his fingers over keys like a puppet master and I watch the people surrender to his sound.

The scrubboard man hits his chest, pounds his spirit out, and gives himself the breath of zydeco. He carries the scrubboard like a mirror, facing the audience as if to remind us that we are all reflected in this music. With the spoon in his hand, he scratches out different rhythms against the surface.

Then the rains finally come down hard on the club's tin roof, adding to the percussion of this place. Nature has come to dance with us tonight. A couple moving near me entwine themselves in a two-step, tethering their arms together, their feet moving in intricate patterns. They turn one another's bodies around, studying them from different vantages as if seeking the finer parts of one another in this dance.

Here, among the diversity of colors and social classes and Cajun and Creole cultures, I see what zydeco is about. I experience the happy, salty snap-bean atmosphere in which these people live: the salt that enhances one's life, enhances what it means to be human.

I stick to the zydeco sound like a fly to a trap, mesmerized by the many worlds that arise from Jeffery's fingertips. As I dance, I collide with its different sounds; the sounds of the farms and prairies of southwest Louisiana.

"I can't control the spirit that comes out of me," one dancer says to another after making quick patterns with his feet. "Let the spirit move me, let the love come out of me," he tells his partner.

Jeffery digs deep inside himself, reaching down to his roots and the environments he was raised in. This is what this music does—it asks us to dig deep inside ourselves, to labor over the things that matter, to reveal our true selves to others. Something I still struggle to do.

There's a whirlwind of musical turnover among the musicians. Everyone on stage shifts into a different role and picks up a different instrument.

Jeffery hands off his accordion to someone he knows in the audience, saying, "He loves to dance, always gets holes in his shoes when dancing, but now, I'm going to make him sing for you all."

This is exactly what the accordion is about: it is a community instrument. It is meant to switch hands and be carried by others.

At around midnight, Jeffery straps on his third and mightiest accordion to end the show. It is an instrument that terrifies him—a heavy three-row with eighty bass keys that plays in the keys of A, E, and E#. "It doesn't have an air button, so you gotta work hard for your air," I remember him telling me in his studio. He beats his accordion onto his chest like a defibrillator that can set his heartbeat right again.

❖

At the end of the night, the musicians huddle in the headlights of Jeffery's car to split their earnings. On our drive home, the bandmates fall asleep in the back seat. Jeffery gets to talking about someone who was present at tonight's show, a friend of his who has a promising future but is struggling with a drug problem and womanizing.

"His white friends are turning him bad, giving him the drugs because they're jealous of his talent and want him destroyed."

Voodoo and vendettas are tearing into these musicians, he tells me. It's a challenge he had to overcome himself as a young musician. "I was a womanizer once. I hurt a lot of people. Music gave me women. I played with Zydeco Force for eighteen years and the best thing I ever did was leave them." He tells me about his drinking, the accidents he got into from driving drunk, almost going to jail for failing his responsibilities as a father. The audience used to throw drugs at him onstage. Other musicians would pocket them; he struggled to kick them back. "I was living bad," he says. It was his wife, Millie, who helped him survive by encouraging him to set goals. "She tells me that 'A man without a vision will perish.'"

Back at Jeffery and Millie's place, everything drops into a deafening silence. The blood of this strong land courses through me. I am moved by the vigor and intensity of life here. This is the kind of hard work that's worth it to me—sweating for your people so that you can help uplift them and bring them home.

I wake the next day to the sounds of KRVS radio hosts Melvin and John blasting from Jeffery's truck. They sign off: "Weather's nice, so *you* be nice. And take care of your kids." I have a quick coffee with Millie before joining her and Jeffery at the discount store to gather supplies for Millie's "Two-Stepping It Into 50" birthday.

Millie's been telling me about how Jeffery becomes a different person when he plays. She wants him to get the palms of his hands tattooed with images of an accordion, "so whenever he feels lost, he can always feel like he's stepping on stage to perform. All he has to do is clasp his hands together."

We're at Andy's Discount Store under the surveillance of many cameras. I tread carefully under signage that warns the shoppers of jail time if they steal.

The life of a zydeco musician is hard and the pandemic only made it tougher by decimating a lot of the work. Jeffery and Millie penny-pinch, living off whatever proceeds they get from his performances. Millie peruses the aisles, feels around for those precious items that will help her two-step into a fantasy where people no longer hurt. When she emerges, she is carrying balloons and a tiara.

◆◆◆◆◆

On my final morning, Jeffery and Millie offer to drive me to the Greyhound station. We slip through the streets of Louisiana as if in reverse time. I thank them for all their work. At a traffic light, a driver in the lane next to us raises his handgun, looks directly at me, releases the magazine, and replaces it with a new one before speeding off around the corner.

My transition back into wandering is always hard on my nerves. I question my motives for moving again; wonder why I am so quick to abandon the familiar. There is a part of me that wants to make my home in stillness. But I also know that stagnancy brings me illness of mind and body.

I am grateful for the things Jeffery Broussard has taught me: that we can live profoundly despite our suffering. That battered hearts can beat more intensely than those closed off to feeling. He has encouraged me to make music of my wounds and to not hold anything back. To trust in the pain I carry and to put it out into the world, where it will resonate with others and honor our communities.

Zydeco is a testimony to those who came before: to the ancestors who toiled in the fields under the hot sun to take care of their families and who shared their resources with one another despite their common hardships. Zydeco is a living lesson to appreciate and respect our past and to continue keeping the rich cultures alive.

I leave Louisiana in a daze, with a lasting impression of the land and its people. I shift into movement once again, in the manner of my elders—aunts, uncles, and grandparents—who traveled long distances to and from Mexico on foot and on buses.

I go via the route of the Great Migration, following the path of the exodus from Louisiana toward Texas and California during the Great Depression. I move on a bus over long stretches of road, keeping the spirits of Jeffery's people close to me, hoping to feel the ghosts of the land still moving about on the prairies and bayous. The rains come down, as they have been for days. Droplets run down the glass of the windows, beating their music while I sway in and out of sleep.

CEREMONY OF CORRIDOS

I FEAR THAT MY PARENTS' SUFFERING HAS PERMEATED EVERY ASpect of my life. That the dark things that haunt them have passed into me by osmosis and might overtake me one day. My fear comes from the environments that persecuted us for our language, our poverty. In the past, my family would look to corridos to alleviate these dark things, to give us a framework for understanding our lives beyond language. Now, in my spare time, I write corridos to free me from these patterns of fear.

I am trying to break our patterns in other ways too. While I am on this journey, I am also approaching another—the journey of fatherhood. I've spent my life collecting the knowledge my parents weren't given the chance to accumulate as migrants. That wherever you go, there you are; that we will never have this life fully figured out, so we should go easy on ourselves; that family is not just found in blood, but in camaraderie. Now, I hope to pass that knowledge onto my boy. I hope to teach him empathy, to see himself in others and in his landscapes. I will teach him to seek the counsel of his ancestors in trees and rivers, as well as in the relatives that abound in our world. I will teach him that family is a state of mind.

As I move through the South along the route of the Great Migration, I think of home. I think of a son who slowly materializes inside his mother's womb, his life force swelling every day. The task of fatherhood is ahead of me and I question what that might entail; what it means to handle the feet of a new spirit runner. I know that already this boy lives in liberation, moves to his own rhythm, swims in the many colors of his spiritual heritage. Already he bathes in the knowledge of his Mexican, Indigenous, and Italian ancestry, holding the mythologies of the Adriatic Sea alongside the folklore of his desert relatives. Already he carries the sacred knowledge that will guide him in life. And I know he will have a lot to teach me. Every day that his mama's stomach gets bigger, my life is given more form and meaning. I await his arrival and hope that no tears will define this baby's life the way they did mine. I watch him kick and stretch inside his mother's womb, fashioning new worlds with his feet, already making space for new dreams.

I move my hands over the sphere of his mother's belly, hoping to shape him with love into something great. But it isn't entirely up to me, I know. A child can be born to repeat the cycles and endure the obstacles his ancestors couldn't conquer. I fear the stories that might get repeated; I fear that the things I couldn't vanquish in my own life might permeate his. So I bathe him in our music, in the rhythms that I hope already touch his heart. I protect him with the vibrations of accordions to welcome him into the ceremony of corridos. The ceremony of story.

CHORUS

"99 YEAR WALTZ"

Ed Poullard (Beaumont, Texas)

THERE WAS A TIME WHEN ACCORDIONS THRIVED IN THE UNITED States. In the late 1800s, the instrument established itself among Creole communities in Louisiana. Then it took root on the West Coast, when Italians settled in San Francisco after the Gold Rush, and spread into the Pacific Northwest, where I reside. Later, there was an explosion of their popularity in Chicago and New York during the Prohibition years.

Everywhere, accordions were giving immigrants the lung power to sing their repressed stories from porches, theaters, and taverns. Back then it was called the squeeze-box and it moved where the migrants took it. Their bellows stretched into the lands that birthed gospel, the Midwest blues, and the boogie-woogies of the South. Wherever they landed, accordions wove together the social fabrics of the time and gave people a way to revolt against oppression.

During World War II, their manufacture was paused. The world's goods were retooled for the war mobilization effort, and most manufacturers were based in Germany and Japan. Later, the instrument entered the sacred circles of bluegrass and helped transform country and western music. Eventually the accordion's sounds entered the swanky clubs of the 1950s and became equated with high-class society. Its sounds brought revolution to rock-and-roll bands in the 1960s, when it also swirled into zydeco music, and moved onward to where Tex-Mex bandas thrived. As the music sutured the border cultures of the United States and Mexico, communities used it to sound the alarm on injustices and bring people together.

Nowadays, accordions seem to exist only in pawn shops or antique shops, collecting dust and passing through the hands of hobbyists. They are seen as fixtures of a time past, their reeds and their stories both grown stale. To try to preserve their ancestral sounds, I travel our eroded landscapes to find the musical alchemists who still play and build accordions. Though I find many players, there are not very many people left in the United States who know how to construct them. The craftsmen I pursue are rare, often elderly, and the last of their kind. These people, who understand the instrument as a tool of working-class life, hold many communities' emotional and spiritual knowledge in their hands.

One place I find hints of this fading way of life is in Beaumont, Texas, among the massive skyline of oil refineries. Here I locate Mr. Ed Poullard, a world-class fiddler and one of the last remaining Black Creole accordion makers.

On the periphery of where Ed lives is an intricate weave of pipelines that hang in the open like metallic entrails, sucking the earth dry. The monstrous mazes gush with the black blood of oil, bleeding mother nature of her life force. Here in the marsh, smokestacks stand tall, like lit-up cigars. Some of the best music in the world has emerged from this land, against a backdrop of clashing ecosystems. As in so many other parts of the United States, this is a land of the persecuted, where people came together around the accordion.

Here in Texas, between the prairies and the bayous and near the state border with Louisiana, Ed has created something special. When he's not playing his fiddle in festivals, he's nestled inside the small shop in his backyard, creating the myriad little pieces that make up the accordion. For someone who's famous for constructing single-row accordions, Ed is a humble man. He dresses in muted colors: the creamy browns of a woodworker, or the UPS colors that he wore during deliveries in his younger days. While the rains marinate the motherland outside, greatness takes place in Ed's workshop, where he assembles the hardware that will help others give voice to their ancestral sounds. His life follows a monastic routine, defined by the working man's spirit he cultivated doing shifts at a chemical plant for over thirty years, hauling slabs of rubber onto conveyor belts by hand. Now, framed pictures show him alongside other famous musicians who swore by the world-class Poullard Accordions. I walk through his shop in awe, observing accordions lying on worktables in varying colors and stages of development. I itch to press their release buttons, freeing the spirits that transmigrate through them.

Ed Poullard, born in 1952, comes from an important family of Creole musicians who have mastered the old styles of playing. He's been a woodworker and cabinet builder all his life, and making accordions was a natural transition for him—one that he made only later in life, though he has been playing accordion since he was about fourteen years old.

"I was afraid of opening them up and seeing what all was

involved on the inside. I didn't want to mess anything up because the accordion I was playing wasn't mine. It was my daddy's. And I wasn't going through anything like that," he says with a laugh.

The instruments are intimidating pieces of hardware. Building an accordion is one of the most complicated woodworking projects one can undertake. It takes over one hundred hours to build a single one, and Ed usually spreads it over a four- to nine-month period. Some of the technical aspects of building a single-row accordion can take a lifetime to master, a process made even more urgent by the speed at which its craftsmen are disappearing. Black accordion makers in the United States are particularly rare. Ed is among the last to hold this knowledge.

The basic parts of a single-row accordion, Ed explains, are essentially a giant harmonica. "A harmonica has ten notes, it's air-driven, but it's air-driven by personal air—by mouth. This," he continues, pointing to an accordion, "this has a bellows to manipulate, to achieve the air drive to make it work. And it's much larger, but basically it operates the same way. It operates with reeds." He brings over a reed system that looks like the bones of a filleted fish, cradling the intricate circuitry between his knees. "This is the inside. It's a pretty complicated little box. Every time you push one of these buttons, four of these reeds sound. And they're loud," he says, laughing. "Very loud. For an acoustic instrument, they're hated by other people that play wooden acoustic instruments. I play the fiddle, and when we get together and sit and start jamming and one of these shows up," he says, lifting the rack of the reeds, "it kinda overcomes the sound we have." He laughs again. "But it's not an unpleasant sound. It's just loud."

Ed didn't start building accordions until his daughter took an interest in playing them. It was then that he realized he was one of the few gatekeepers to this traditional music and began tinkering. But when it came to assembling an entire instrument, he didn't know where to start. He did a lot of things on his own, like building his own keyboard, but could never get it right until he made a few trips out to learn from his famous friend, Marc Savoy. Savoy is one of the original builders of the Cajun accordion in Louisiana. Over the years, he has helped Ed improve his craft.

"I have original faceplates that he gave me with the measurements already spelled out on them," Ed says. Faceplates are the pieces of hardware that pinpoint the exact locations of buttons so the player can achieve the perfect sound. He stands up to fetch them, showing me the faceplates but not their measurements. Trade secrets. "He don't do that for anyone, but he did that for me. And this was thirty years ago."

The accordion, he says, has been manufactured in Louisiana since the 1960s. The first person to create them in the region, Sidney Brown—also recognized as the first Cajun accordion maker—pioneered experimentation with existing instruments. He created new frames and parts for the accordion and used whatever scraps he could to make it work. The result was that accordions became more functional and longer lasting.

Ed motions to the two accordions he's currently working on with an apprentice. His teaching technique works by call and response, like juré, bonding one maker to another, as well as to the eventual player and to the broader community. To build an accordion is to build and rebuild a relationship, solidifying the spiritual in the physical.

To build an accordion from scratch, Ed says, you need a vision—a color scheme, or a concept. Much of the process, like cutting the materials, is repetition. The bellows are all usually the same size and, depending on the manufacturer, so are the reeds. He brings out an assortment of pieces from several cabinets, laying parts down before me one by one. He sifts through them like a puzzle. His first step involves the slide plates—a thin piece of wood with the dimensions of a book and the thickness of a potato chip, cut to hold four equally thin, bookmark-shaped pieces that slide up and down. He shows me how the slide plate attaches to the keyboard block, which connects to metal rods and knobs that manipulate the slide plate. He pushes down on one of the four knobs, which are known as stops. "All that does is close off that row, so air cannot go across the reeds. This has to be done with the utmost precision, because it affects your air. You don't want any air leaks when the instrument is complete.

"After all this is done, I will take some veneer and I spray the end plates, or dye them. Then I engrave the design on the plates. Before I add all the slide plate's mechanisms to it, I drill the surface holes on both plates."

What he's described so far is about a month and a half's work. "The next part takes about a week—it's building this keyboard, and this base box, and cutting out the framework. And the glue time." While he waits between steps, he might play an instrument. Today, he brings down his father's fiddle and plays the "99 Year Waltz," sometimes known as "The Convict's Waltz" or "The Old Carpenter's Waltz." His fingers quiver over the old strings. I feel the fiddle's wails in my chest.

Ed uses mainly domestic materials, but he shows me an accordion he built from wood imported from Africa and South America. He tries to stick with domestic wood as much as possible because he can trust the source. When woods of unknown origin are cut, he tells me, they can create toxic clouds of dust.

"I try to discourage people from dyeing anything but curly maple—it's a wood that's really enhanced when dye is applied to it. It just pops." I put my fingers on the cherry wood, noticing how it gives the accordion a specific visual signature. When dye is applied, the wood gets darker over time.

After he's finished with the wood, Ed lets the instrument cure like tobacco for about a week in a climate-controlled room before assembling the parts—installing the plates on the treble side, gluing things into place. "A lot of that stuff you just can't see looking at [the] accordion. People don't have a clue what's going on on the inside."

Then he starts working on the frame—putting corner supports onto the bellow frames as well as the treble and bass ends. Gluing those together takes a long time. Then, he test-fits it to clamps to prepare for the bellows.

He pauses before explaining any further. Precision at this stage is essential. "Once you glue that crap together," he says, chuckling, "you might as well throw it away if you're not gonna get it right. I don't like throwing stuff away, and I might as well quit the things I don't intend on doing right the first time." Poullard has had to throw away only two accordions in his life. "The second time, I said, 'there will be no more mistakes.'"

He's hard on himself. Perhaps too hard. But it is a merciless industry, and his accordions demand the absolute best of him. I am moved by his commitment to perfection. He grabs a piece of the keyboard and scrutinizes it.

"This is a pain," he says, laughing, "a real pain." The parts are burdensome, but as a whole, they reveal the true beauty of the form: "It sure is nice when you get one built and it looks like this."

There is a personal lesson in the craftsmanship too. To me, the accordion is a visual reminder that when we learn to work all the parts of ourselves in unison—our ancestry, our stories, our passions, our fears—they can bring harmony to our lives and help make us whole again.

In Poullard's workshop, we also talk about genre. The original pronunciation of zydeco, he says, was "haricot." The name only changed when the music started to get commercialized and journalists misheard—and misused—the original term.

"That's where the word got twisted. They were coming down here and listening to Clifton Chenier, a long, long time ago." As in Louisiana, where I met with Jeffery, the snap bean is a local vegetable that has lent its name to popular house dances.

"Those house dances were a big part of keeping this tradition alive all these years. Because when the music was dying off, about to become extinct, what they call the prairie community, that really kept that music alive."

In the final stages of accordion assembly, he glues the bellows to the frames, which has to be done very slowly. He puts weights on top of it and lets it sit overnight until it's got a good bond on it. Any air holes must be sealed with glue. Then he has to make and size the reed blocks for whatever key the instrument will be in. He pulls out a handful of reed blocks from a drawer to show me. They look like haircombs. The length of the reeds will vary, but their width will all be the same.

"Larry Miller [a Cajun accordion maker from L.A.] told me there's over six hundred individual pieces of wood that goes into one of these things. When you look at it, you think, nah, no way. But every individual piece . . . there's this one, this one, this one." He loses count of what's in his hand and laughs. "I do whatever it takes to get it done and if I had to stop to think about, 'man I got a lot of pieces to cut out,' I'd never build these damn things, there ain't no way." Finally, he cuts metal for tuning.

Single-row accordions, like the ones Ed builds, are widely used in French Canadian music as well as Irish, Cajun, and zydeco. Ed tells me that there are only a few Tex-Mex musicians who play the single-row accordion. "Santiago Jiménez Jr. plays one. He has one of these Acadian accordions that he got from Marc Savoy a long time ago. A guy named Josh Baca, from Los Texmaniacs, I [also] built him a single-row accordion. His uncle is Max Baca—one of the best bajo sexto players in the country."

Ed had open-heart surgery last year, which slowed him down for eight months. The episode was a reminder that there is no one for Ed to pass his work onto, no one to carry the tradition forward. No one in his family is interested, he says. "I did my duty as a musician and as a father. I taught my kids how to play and I built them each an accordion. Now if they want something else, I'll build it for them, but they gotta start using them three they got," he says, laughing. "Nobody's coming up in my family that's interested in doing this. A lot of people that want to learn, none of them live around here." He has some guys in the area who work offshore, who come in for a week here and there to learn to build accordions before they travel again. But it's hard to take in an apprentice with a schedule like that. Building accordions is a long-term commitment.

"It's a big job. It's dangerous for someone who doesn't have the right attitude," Ed says. "The tools that you use, you gotta know how to build jigs, and all kinds of other little goodies to use to keep from cutting your fingers off. Most of the time you can't wear gloves."

For Ed, to play the accordion is to size up the mess of what it means to be human and to express that humanness in a way that brings him order and harmony. By way of bass and treble, he articulates the reconciliation of body and spirit, life and death. Tucked between the folds of the bellows is a way to contend with life and answer to the violent circumstances that people like myself have been thrust into.

I am moved by the discipline that Ed Poullard brings to his work and the parameters he has drawn for living with purpose. The methodical nature of his craft, his ability to bring forth so much life from inanimate objects, his relentless pursuit of the archaic—these things inspire me. Nowadays, with so many competing demands for our attention, I feel a sort of serenity among old souls like him, who know what it's like to stick with things long term.

I can't help but see a bit of my father in Ed. Both men remind me of the value of commitment, of applying ourselves to the things that matter and pursuing them to their end. There's sadness in this comparison too because I am reminded of all the ways I couldn't stick with the things my father wanted for me as a kid—and still can't, like his ideas of masculinity, or the notion that we must endure the hard rules placed upon us without complaint. Ed Poullard is a painful reminder of how my father wanted me to be, and how I am not.

I leave Poullard's workshop and look out over the Texas horizon. I inhale and hold my breath over this land, keeping this land's magic contained deep inside my lungs. Then I exhale, releasing a bit of my own spirit and preparing for the next stop on my journey for true sound: San Antonio's conjunto scene.

THE DREAMWORLD

IN THE ONLY PHOTO I HAVE OF MY GRANDFATHER, HE'S DRESSED IN manta and wearing a straw hat, standing with family members and smiling as he holds an accordion. My father gave the photo to me. I'm in it too, swinging on a rope, too young to remember the moment it was taken.

As a boy, I used to take a radio up into a tree to be alone with music and to summon my grandfather's spirit. I knew that he spent many of his days and nights suspended in a hammock, so I would climb the apple trees to try to access a similar experience, adrift in the middle space between the sky and the ground.

"Abuelo," I would ask, "in what ways am I tied to you?"

In answer, the winds that rustled around me would drop fruit to smash down on the ground, amid the mush of other fallen fruits that already buzzed with flies.

According to my family, my grandfather was an odd, eccentric man whose story deserved no further investigation. They said he lived only in the dreamworld of his mind and spent his days swaying his life away in his hammock. Even as a child, I could sense a distance in the stories people told of him; I could tell from the way they spoke about him that he might have caused them some hurt. I knew there was some shame in speaking his name and that the scraps they revealed of him hinted at someone who was wild and on his own path.

But he was also blood. I knew that his wild ways might manifest in me in some form and I feared what that could mean. At times I wanted to face that truth; at other times I wasn't ready. I knew what my family thought of my grandfather but I needed to know what my grandfather knew, or thought he knew, about our family. I worried that his fears and his qualms, our qualms, were inheritable and incurable. By learning more about him, I wanted to know—and didn't want to know— what was in store for me.

When I pressed relatives to tell me more about him, they waved me away. "He's just a crazy man dreaming up crazy things." Even though they were dismissive, something about this description resonated with me. My grandfather was different, doing things differently, and I sensed he might be onto something. I needed to know that there were people in my bloodline who were taking bold action to live a different way, pursuing fantasies and dreams in a world that deprived us of so much. I couldn't hold a grudge against another dreamer. All those years I lived in Yakima, dreams were what kept me going.

Up in the tree, I hear my mother calling. I tear an apple free

and I hop to the ground with it in my hand. I devour it and toss
the core to the birds.

—————

Various times, I tried to piece together the fragments I had heard
about my grandfather. That he pursued obsessions like recover-
ing the fabled Spanish gold that was lost in a shipwreck off the
coast of San Juan de Alima. That he loved tortillas, Coca-Cola,
and cigarettes. That he worked as a movie projectionist in a theater in Pomona, California, a job that filled his mind with the
false promises of this land.

This image in particular stayed with me: I imagined him
always alone and in the dark, cracking open film reels like cans
of tuna and consuming the adventures of men who were freer
than him, dreaming himself a better world than the one he had
to endure. I imagined him using the movies to fill the gaps in
his life, giving them his own interpretations and perhaps even
confusing those stories with his own. And I saw myself in him,
because as a child, I did this too—I pretended that I lived inside
of movies, rewriting their stories as I watched, hoping the edited
versions would heal whatever wounds I carried.

I also imagine the sadness my grandfather might have felt
as he struggled to make sense of his circumstances. He probably
carried a lot of shame for abandoning his family and being unable to take on the burdens of migrant life. I must believe that
he still carries the pain of that failure inside him. Now, in his old
age, he probably cannot escape from it. As he lies on his hammock, he must still be hounded by the lives he left behind for
his adventures; by the people who were crushed by the migrant
life he led. Through him, I too am hurting. I too am causing
destruction by always being on the move.

Sometime in the early 1970s, when my grandfather lived in San Diego, he would spend his days working on a marina, helping to mend boats. By night, he slept inside them. I imagined him in the dark, summoning spirits with his accordion, putting his hands to corridos to quell his pain over the people he'd disappointed.

I envisioned him sleeping inside the cabins of these boats, stringing words into songs that would be as close to a confession as someone like him could muster—lyrics that would have explained why he does what he does, why he is who he is. I have to believe that he conjured the memory of his son whom he left to go hungry in Mexico; that maybe he pleaded for forgiveness. I have to believe that a father never forgets his children, that his flesh is permanently on fire with feeling for his kids.

I can hear his music play as the boat thrashes against the coastal waves that rock the marina, his mind darkened by a past that never goes away. I feel the sorrow of such a life and I pursue it by playing music of my own. I wonder if this is as close to the past as I can get, as near to closure as I can find.

THE SOUND OF THE COWS THROUGH THE SOIL

"WHY DO YOU PLAY SO MANY SAD SONGS?" MY FRIEND ASKS, WHEN I send him clips of the ones I'm learning to play.

"To engage in something real for once," I tell him. What I don't tell him is that I also do it to placate and tame my sadness. But he understands, I feel, without my having to say so. After all, we're both from Yakima—the Palm Springs of Sadness. The music I'm learning to play on the accordion is becoming a kind of cold compress to bring down the swelling inside me. It's also my way of relinquishing the notion that I know anything about anything—but I don't tell my friend that part either.

I position my computer in front of a mirror to better imitate the video I'm watching of the ambidextrous Italian accordion player Massimo Romeo Craveri. He is the latest addition to my library of musicians whose playing exhibits the depth of their capacity to feel. I collect sounds like theirs—ones that capture what I think a soul ought to sound like if it escaped our bodies.

Massimo's videos take me to Italy, where I watch him embrace a song called "Nadiejda," by the late French composer Stéphane Delicq, who was Massimo's teacher and friend. I observe Massimo's movements as he feels his way through the song; how he sways; how, with closed eyes, he appears to be living through deep personal experiences. In the moment, his music seems to be more powerful to him than sight. I want music to mean something that powerful to me.

This is what I look for when I seek out makers and players, from Jeffery Broussard to Massimo: the deep, personal connection between a person and their accordion.

I resolve to learn "Nadiejda" and grapple with the song in stages spread out over several weeks. As I move through it note by note, as the notes begin to form a melody, I experience bursts of cold shudders across my body. I feel something alive crawling over my skin. I often have these small physical awakenings when learning songs. This alone is enough motivation to keep at the instrument. I play through the notes, I unite the right and left hands, and I try to leave space for whatever emotions come to the surface. I try to make music as much of a spiritual experience as possible.

Throughout, I am guided by Massimo's playing. It's evident that he is someone whom other men can learn from—men who do not yet know how to express what they feel. Men like me. Massimo's music carries the potential for a different, better masculinity. He sounds out the notes that hurt him and sutures them into something good. He strikes at the tender parts of himself, freed from the burden of always having to appear strong. It's my hope that by sitting with people like him, I will also learn to confront these things in myself.

Inspired by his playing, I muster up the strength to ask Massimo for a virtual interview. He appears on my screen, a man with long white hair and a white beard. As he filters his Italian through the choppy medium of Spanish, we do our best to navigate the common language between us.

Massimo is an elder and a recluse who lives in the mountains of northern Italy, where the accordion also has a robust history and presence. He retreated from the disappointments of city life to farm in the mountains north of Torino, where he raises goats and sheep and makes cheese and fine music.

"Soy un ciudadano arrepentido," he says, searching for the right images to explain himself. "I left the city fifteen years ago [out of] necessity to live in the heights among the clouds." The constant city noise, the quantity of people, was making him sick. "I felt suffocated. Not a tranquil life—difficult to lead a calm life and hard to reflect in the city." In line with his political values, he also raises rabbits to feed the poor villagers and workers. He walks the streets showcasing his rabbits and butchering them on the spot to help poor families who cannot afford the higher market prices.

I notice he sits at the foot of a statue—Ganesha, the Hindu deity—and ask him about it.

He turns to his deity. "An elephant with a rat. That they're friends is incredible," he says. He is compelled by how two seemingly opposite species can make peace and thrive in harmony. If only we could embody those teachings in our lives, we'd be better for it, he says. In his youth he was influenced by Indian philosophy, but now his spiritual forces come from nonreligious places. "There is nothing better than a plant, the sky, the rain. My spirituality is in these things. My spirituality is in the sound. This is why I cry when I play, because I'm having a spiritual experience with my accordion."

He tells me that the accordion initially came to him in a

dream. "Back in the day, accordions used to be very popular and I would sit for hours hearing this music in the streets. But I did not know the theory then and I still don't know music theory now. I learned by watching and listening and playing."

Ultimately, Massimo believes that the player must give himself to his instrument. "He donates sentiment to it, the origin of most sacred things," he says. "When I play music, many times I must restrain myself. I say, 'debo detenerme' [I must stop]. But then I feel a knot in the throat and often I begin to cry." He looks down for a minute. "I am alone, I play alone. I play very profound music. There are some times that I can't play due to so much emotion." When he doesn't know the source of what he's feeling, he plays what he cannot utter in words.

Similarly, I try to write what I cannot yet come to say aloud. I sometimes feel as alone as Massimo does, and I muster up what strength I can to access and express what I feel. To do what I can to bring more sentiment into the world.

◆◆◆◆◆

I reach out to another player who, like me, is devoted to the Castagnari accordion. His name is Simone Bottasso. While he currently lives in the Netherlands, he is originally from a small village in the Northern Italian mountains between Torino and France, the region that borders the Alps. It's a town where, he tells me, "Unfortunately, 'musicians' are not the work parents expect from their sons."

When he speaks, Bottasso is pensive and philosophical. He is suspicious of logic or definitions that box things into simple concepts. Instead, he feels the constant desire to perceive things in a new way and to do so through new experiences. To him, instruments provide an opportunity to access a rich diversity of spiritual, emotional, and intellectual encounters. As he searches for critical points of view that challenge everything he thought he knew, he also tries to capture this element in music.

"For me, it's not enough to make people emotional. I have a need to express something beyond music, beyond words," he says. Like Massimo, he grieves the mundaneness of our lives and the way we get stuck in predictable patterns, and he sees music as a means of defying them. But he is more interested in music's capacity for novel discovery than just as a means of emotional expression.

The accordion also offers Bottasso a way to find peace within the chaos of the world. During the COVID-19 shutdowns, when his inability to see his family was giving him nightmares, playing music grounded him by offering a mantra that helped him heal. He made a habit of focusing on different sounds, toggling between them like a stick shift. "The accordion transforms my world when everything seems to be collapsing."

His aim is to create beauty and then amplify it for others to experience. As a small boy, he played the accordion from his parents' balcony, casting his melodies like spells over the village. Up there, level with the birds, he directed his music toward lonely passersby, hoping that if they felt isolated from other people, the sounds would make them feel connected again. He synced himself to the pulse of the village, playing in the direction of cathedrals, cafes, and corridors. He used sound to feel his way through its streets. He rubbed his fingers raw as he committed more songs to memory. The accordion became an extension of himself. "Without it," he says now, "I am nothing."

Despite the instrument's importance to him now, he struggled to embrace it growing up. It was not considered "real" because it was a folk instrument, perceived as being too working class. These days, part of his experimentation with sound comes from his desire to restore people's wearied relationship to the instrument and in doing so to reestablish their connection to the elders. He describes his devotion to playing as "trying to take revenge in the name of the accordion."

The accordion also offers him a very personal connection to his heritage. Like me, he hears his grandfather in his sound. Bottasso recalls the sweet sounds of country life, when he used to visit his grandfather's farm. As a young boy, he loved putting his ears to the ground to absorb what the cows might sound like through the soil, which is rich with sounds, he says. The country filled him with wisdom as he played with the cowbells, rolled in the grass, and sat outdoors with his grandfather over fresh food.

Now, as an adult, Bottasso uses sounds as a way to reengage with the past. Along with smells, sounds have the capacity to unlock deep stories inside him, and he speaks about them with a sort of sadness. Music, for him, is a gesture of respect to these sensory experiences—good moments lived among good people on pristine landscapes; the love and hard work that goes into the land; the delicate balance and interdependence between man, animal, and nature.

"This way of life takes proper nurturing," he says. "Take care of the cows and they in turn sustain village life." Likewise, if you take care of your music, it will sustain your people.

His father also helped cultivate Bottasso's attentiveness to the quality of sound, taking him to the mountains to climb and pay attention to nature's soundscapes. "My father helped me to find pleasure in sounds. To listen to the small breaths in everything." His father, a plumber, would also encourage Bottasso to regard his work as a form of music making. "'See?' my father would say, indicating the pipes of his profession. 'My tubes also make music. You should come work with me.'"

But even though Bottasso wishes to honor the past, he is not interested in preserving it through his music. "I don't want to live in the world of my father," he says. "I'm making new stuff." His work is a reminder that there is liberation in experimenting.

We must maintain our obsession with sounds, he advises, with hearing one another and hearing one another out. "The moment you decide to pay attention and dedicate your time to watching and to listening, your life changes."

GETTING BACK YOUR COLOR

LONG AGO IN ANOTHER LIFE, AS AN UNDERGRADUATE, I TOOK A TRIP TO NORTHERN Ireland to study the Troubles, moving between the sorrows of Catholic and Protestant communities to collect their stories. One night, after a long coastal drive, slumbering under heavy emotions even then, I stumbled into a village set along thrashing shores alive with bitter winds. In an obscure local tavern, a former gathering place for IRA militants, I ordered a Harp Lager. As I sat and drank and deepened my connection to the soul of the land, a group of local fishermen pulled me out of whatever brewed inside of me. They retrieved traditional instruments from behind the bar and began to tell the stories of lives lost during the Troubles. It was here that I learned how other people mourned with music, and where I was first ensnared by the sounds of the

Irish accordion, also known as the melodeon. The sound of it burrowed deeply inside me and never left. I vowed to return.

Several weeks after my interviews with Massimo and Bottasso, I return to the music of Ireland and the U.K. by reaching out to accordionists who live there. The name of the first player I speak to is Will Pound, a musician from the English Midlands. He has performed extensively across the country, including for Prince Harry at Buckingham Palace.

I ask him what power the instrument holds for him.

"I do it to reinvent myself out of my depression," he says. "The accordion is a good distraction. It stops the bad thoughts. I've [also] written my best music when depressed."

His playing refuses to conform to any one musical genre. "It fascinates me to put two styles together," he says. He sees this as a way of connecting listeners who might otherwise be drawn to different kinds of music.

Pound also sees color in his music, a phenomenon known as synesthesia.

On-screen, he pulls up his accordion for me to see. "I see this melodeon not as light brown, but more as a purple-green. If I play something [as] bright as the note of A," he says, pausing to play the note, "I see green in my head." He continues to play me different colors. "Something purple, [like] C minor, is a bit darker and richer," he says. "A major chord, it's a bit more bright. G is quite bright green. D is a deep red—blood-vessel red. E minor seventh chord is a dark violet, quite dark."

Depression, he says, has a black-brown color to it. "To a certain degree, also white, because you're blinded by its white noise." And with black, you can't see your way through, he adds. He tells me that the colors he sees can change depending on the chord and on his state of mind. What he chooses to play also depends on his mood—"I write music that's opposite to my emotion because that's where I want to be," he says.

He tells me about his work bringing music to patients in intensive care units and to children in a poor ex-mining community in Wales. In London, he plays for people who have been unhoused, using his synesthesia to try to find songs and sounds that will speak to the listener directly.

He recalls a particular story about a meeting with a former banker who had lost everything. "He lived in a train station and I played bright-colored stuff for him. Brass stuff. I played lots of fat chords for him," he says, as if to feed and nourish him. "My music brought him back home."

It's also, in its way, what music did for him. Music resuscitated him, literally giving him the breath he needed after he underwent two open-heart surgeries when he was four years old.

"I was given a chance to live by my doctors. I took up the harmonica to help me with my breathing."

What Will pursues in his work is what I also hope music will offer me—a ticket back home. I want the power to see brightness in places that feel dark, the way Will can. I want to look at the world and see it painted in scales and musical chords—to see my writing as a palette of colors that has the ability to bring about a new world.

—◆◆◆◆◆—

Somewhere on the edges of no-man's-land, an Irish musician wanders through forgotten places. David Munnelly is an accordionist from County Mayo, Ireland, who has made it his purpose to find his proper place in an ancient Celtic land. He feels the power of his people in the peat he walks on. As he walks over the bog, he looks into the horizon and upon a world where, he says, people understand red wine more than they understand music.

I make my long-awaited return to Ireland, and that mesmerizing Irish accordion sound, by meeting with him virtually. He speaks to me from a room along a bay that is beat back by strong ocean winds. Running his fingers through the grain of his beard, Munnelly tells me how, when he plays music, he thinks of its message in "big fucking letters."

As David Munnelly maneuvers over his lands, stepping through the sacred places that hold his ancestral past, he's always in search of the stories trapped inside dilapidated structures—houses that have been abandoned to the bogs, to be forgotten and consumed by nature. He tells me of one house he wandered into that sat near an ancient creek and had fallen into disrepair. Inside, he found a box. Within the box were some songs written by an old priest. In these songs, he found bits of himself.

His journey, as he sees it, is to excavate himself from the many past lives buried in the landscape. "My job is to bring those songs back to life," he says to me, "because my belief is that we've been here before."

David Munnelly comes from a long lineage of musicians, people who gathered around the fireplace to warm themselves with the music of their ancestors. His grandmother was his mentor. "My grandmother grew up believing that music was religion. I didn't go to music school. I learned in front of an open fire inside the house, and listened to my grandmother." They often played together with neighbors. "Between two houses we had about fifteen instruments."

While lights from passing boats and towers penetrate his room with red and blue rays, he tells me about the importance of leaning into the sounds of life, plugging into our surroundings as a mode of healing.

"In Ireland, people kept going after surviving the famine. What gets me by is believing that I can get through this"—the sadness of the daily struggle. On his nature walks he moves with intention, careful not to disturb the resting places of his ancestors or pop the delicate layer of peat that separates him from the underworld. This is also how I imagine him handling his music: delicately, carefully, always informed by the spirits around him.

His lifelong experience with music offers a constant possibility of transformation and evolution. "Truly there's more that can be done. There must be something different than who I am. Maybe I want to say something else." I share this sentiment. Because words can sometimes fail us, melody can save us, he says. It can give you back your color, give you back your feelings, and give back the stories that migrants lose on dangerous pilgrimages. All we have to do is pay attention to that drive to express ourselves.

Munnelly moves his fingers over his accordion like he moves over landscapes—to prove that he, and all of his people, are worthy of something. "That's why my people have traveled the world like weeds," he says. "They worked all over the place because they had to. That is my tradition, to create, invent your own ideas. That's something the Irish were very good at doing. For me it's about rehashing the tradition beyond the labels and creating new sound, new energy."

He pulls his hands apart, stretching the bellows of his accordion. Between his hands he carries the power of two worlds and will keep moving restlessly between them.

"When we play the tunes of our elders, we're bringing back their personalities," Munnelly tells me. "I'm bringing them back to life when I play old music. In every country, in music, people are honoring the dead."

This is how it is for me too, I tell him. "In Mexico, people mourn with monarch butterflies that embody the dead. They are resurrected in their vibrant colors. Mourning is a communal celebration." The accordion is the medium through which to have a conversation with the spirit of my past. I study its parts, its grain, its design, searching for the source of its magic to connect with my history and create new stories.

UNEXPECTED PLACES

I THINK BACK TO MY TIME IN HIGH SCHOOL, AT A PARRANDA IN YAKIMA, where I sat alone over a beer. In the memory, I am tucked in a dark corner in the back, watching the ground thunder with boots and dancing bodies, while my fingers mimic the movements of the accordionist onstage. This is the kind of festive night my grandfather loved, the sort he moved through in the tabernas of Mexico and California. Out of the music, I pull my grandfather's spirit and ask him to sit beside me for a drink. He's barely present—his energy is faded and he keeps looking over his shoulder, as if at the thing that has always pursued him.

"What haunts you so much, Abuelo?"

The intensity of the music moves through us and I cannot draw any words from him. He is focused on the smoke and lights and I see his mind moving elsewhere, his desire to return to the amorphous shape of the dancers.

Does he not see me, sitting next to him on the barstool and swimming in a haze of drink, desperately looking for a way out of this hard town? Instead of making a life for myself and my family somewhere softer, I am still here, once again resorting to the darker corners where there are no good ghosts, no clear shapes, no clear answers. I have invoked the idea of my grandfather, but right now, he is incapable of offering me guidance.

My hold on him slips; my connection to the music dies down. I slam back to this desolate place and push away from the bar. I cut through the crowd, inching forward until I escape through a door and into the alleyway. Here, at the Knights of Columbus dance hall, the men used to gather in summer. Battles sometimes occurred, obscured by the loud music; bandas meant to resolve disputes between men who worked long days in the fields and factories. Here in the alleyways, and sometimes even inside on the dance floors, men were made to answer for their violations to the social order or to the ways of our people. They were reminded that in this world there is always someone bigger than you.

Now in adulthood, after my move back to Washington, I return to this now shuttered salón. I lean near trash bins against the wall of the alley, fanning sweat from my shirt. I think of my elders who met out here many times, in dance and in the dead of night, who have now passed. In this dirty alleyway next to a junkyard lot, I eulogize the counsel of these men. The cigarette butts and bottle caps littering the ground are mementos of a lost time, one filled with people who made the best of their impoverished conditions. I stand here now because I couldn't as a kid. Back then, I wasn't able to understand what these men endured. But now, as an adult, I live with that same drive inside me: to save my people from this town. To save them from themselves.

Dance halls make manifest the despair that I carry in my accordion, the agonizing sound that I return to in my playing that takes me back to my younger days. Dance halls were for festive times, but they were also a way to answer to your darkness. The hard-hitting lyrics of corridos and the vigor of the movements stoked men's tempers and drew out their pain on the dance floor. These places were for relinquishing your baggage and emerging cleansed. As a child, I would see the pain of men who came to dance give way to wilder emotions. Their celebrations often came to blows. It was just their way.

These men formed my earliest ideas of masculinity. They were men who suffered the harshness of two lands: Yakima and Mexico. These relatives took care of me as a boy, becoming tough so that I wouldn't have to and absorbing the violence so that I might escape it. I carry their violent landscapes inside of me and try to bring them their peace with music.

I touch the old walls of this shuttered salón in Yakima, searching for the vibrations of corridos past. I'm here because I still fear these ghosts. I'm afraid I've failed them by not becoming the man they needed me to become. I could have thanked them more for being my teachers. I feel the walls for the textures of their memories, missing the men that made me. No amount of paint could ever obscure the pain and joy that this place held for me. I am thankful for places like this that safeguarded our story, preserved my people during the tumultuous years, when they were persecuted for being migrants.

PASADITAS

I CONTINUE TO TEACH MYSELF SONGS BY WATCHING MASSIMO PLAY.
In many of his videos his face and fingers are obscured, cross-hatched by filters that seem to insist I live only in his sound, free of distractions.

I am learning to play a song called "Fellini," by Massimo's mentor Stéphane Delicq. I imitate whatever gestures I can from Massimo's obscured figure. But I struggle to mimic the perfect flow of his playing, struggle even to experience ecstasy the way he seems to. I know that to play with the passion Massimo does, I must find my own reasons to feel. I must dig into my own story to help me drive at this instrument, bringing to bear on it the experiences that have propelled me my whole life. As I play,

I repeat the movements I imagine ancestors took with music, inserting the pasaditas and adornos, the personal ornamentations. Losing myself in these lessons gives me a new way to experience my memories of Yakima and reevaluate what I thought I knew of my hometown: that it was a dead-end place for dreams, desolate in color, and full of depressing things. Perhaps even that by ending up there, my people had quit the fight and had been beaten. In retrospect, the person that had been beaten and lost his color was probably me. Now, I reteach myself how to look upon it more generously.

Losing myself in the instrument also gives me a new way to collect the fragments of my grandfather's story. Over the years, another rumor I heard about him was that he worked as a detective in Mexico City. There, in the ink wash of noir, the lines between good and bad deeds sometimes blurred. I envisioned him moving in the hazy atmospheres of gangster underworlds, a cool, crisp observer in a suit and a fedora, peering between the folds of Spanish newspapers or the slats of shadowy blinds. I imagined the clandestine work he might have done tackling jobs on the streets of el Distrito Federal, sweeping up gangsters, interrogating men in alleyways whose deeds may have mirrored some of his own.

I imagined him leaning against brick walls, studying the big city, moving about like the devil himself and making deals to save his own soul. Even as I try to move with him, so many details about him are inaccessible to me.

It's possible that everything that I know and have said about Mexico is wrong. Perhaps so is everything that I know and have said about my family, and everything that I know and have said about myself. I must live with the knowledge that certain truths are inaccessible to me; that sometimes, these imagined scenes are as deep as I can go. I must learn to see things as they are and to acknowledge that perhaps I am sometimes the source of my own pain. What I pursue may only be materializations of the demons working inside me. My job is to bring them out of their shadows and vanquish them.

Most of all, I must overcome this idea that my grandfather represents the whole answer, that the actions of any one person could unite my shattered pieces and make them whole again. Still, I pursue the fragments, following my grandfather's clacking shoes down a dark alley, when suddenly I am slammed into a wall and warned to keep away from a ghost that doesn't want to be pursued.

━━━

Later, I would learn that my grandfather played the accordion upside down, against the natural order of things. But then, that made sense. His world was an inverted one. It was natural for him to come at things differently, to tilt things on their axes. He turned the instrument's power inward, turned its beauty onto himself. And so, the next time I unlock my accordion from its case and strap it to myself, I invert it like he did. I try again to view the world from his perspective. Technically, it is possible to play the instrument this way. But it feels contorted, twisted, like the person I was sometimes told he was. When I press sounds from it, it produces deeper, darker tones than the ones I'm used to producing. The music is too dizzying to keep up and I set the accordion down amid the swirl of vertigo.

The truth remains: My grandfather chose to strike out and live his life differently. I too must find another way to live.

FOR THE PERSON WHOSE WIFE HAS LEFT HIM

(San Antonio)

DAYS AFTER MY TRIP TO BEAUMONT, TEXAS, I RIDE YET ANOTHER Greyhound bus to visit the music scene in San Antonio, a town that sits at the center of extreme ecosystems. To the east, pine country. To the north, hill country. To the south, tropical valleys and palm trees. To the west, desert. These are the environments that converge in the spirit of the people, who come together to make the music of conjunto. San Antonio's uniquely Tejano sound reached Yakima long before I was born. Now, I have come to the city to immerse myself in it, to see what gave root to so much of the music in the region where I grew up.

In the early 1900s, long before my parents settled in the Yakima Valley, Texans were settling in this area to do agricultural work. Among them arrived a famous man—an apple picker like my parents—who, in the 1930s, helped to cement the famous accordion and bajo sexto (sixth bass) ensemble that is now common in both norteño and Texas conjunto music (two popular genres of music that originated in northern Mexico and the southwestern United States). He was Santiago Almeida, a Tejano who partnered with the pioneering conjunto accordionist, Narciso Martínez—who would go on to establish himself as the father of conjunto music.

Almeida left his Texas homeland in the 1950s to settle the dairy town of Sunnyside, in the Yakima Valley, as a campesino. He developed his musical prowess as he worked among our apple trees, experiencing the land as we would go on to do in later decades. He let the land convey to him truths only made clear to beaten-down laborers. I imagine him enveloped by canopies of trees that may still stand today, counting down the days until the hard life subsided for a moment to let him bask in good music and good cuentos (stories). I see him letting the land course deeply through him, the way it did for me. I imagine him finding peace from labor only in the tales he told, in which he imagined scenarios where our people finally persevered.

Between work shifts, Almeida taught his music to other campesinos in the Yakima Valley, planting the seed for many generations of songs to arise from our land. These complicated rhymes of working-class life helped to create the atmospheres that I felt drawn to as a boy, through which I tried linking myself to a past my parents sometimes preferred I did not know. Corridos were an entry point into talking about deeper things in our history—but it was a conversation my parents weren't always ready to have.

The father of conjunto, Narciso Martínez, had no formal education. He worked in the fields, at a zoo feeding animals, and as a trucker. His poverty, transience, and illiteracy kept him grounded in the realities of his people. These circumstances also informed his music: he made his living playing from dirty borrowed accordions until he made enough money to buy his own. As he moved among laborers, he found music in his migrant ways, capturing the folk ambience of the proletariat.

In the 1920s, in San Antonio and along the border towns of Texas and Mexico, the ideas that accordion music espoused were considered dangerous by the upper class for how they threatened the social order of the time. Conjunto and norteño music aired the grievances of the working class, uniting them under a set of beliefs and inspiring them with narratives of heroic revolutionaries—some of which dated as far back as the Mexican Revolution. The music was loud and gritty. Because of the sound's origins and contents, the wealthier classes perceived it as low-class, dirty, vulgar, and suitable only for the cantinas (the bars of Mexican laborers).

Accordions expressed the pain of people who were hurting and adrift on their land. Both the instruments and the music they played provided safe havens for Mexicans and Tex-Mex communities alike—anyone looking to shake off their hard day's labor through dance. Conjuntos means "to gather," and in Texas, this is exactly what it did: it unified the restless, working-class people through a music that asserted their place in history. Because of this history, I feel a sense of unity with the Texas sounds that have passed through Yakima and informed the lives of our campesinos.

—————

My first experience of San Antonio's conjunto culture begins along "the Strip" outside the old Salute Bar—the former home of many conjunto events and a regular venue for conjunto legends like Flaco Jiménez. The bar is on North St. Mary's Street. When I get to the front steps, the first thing I do is cross the street to explore the alleyways along East Russell Place. I'm pulled away from the gentrification of the Strip and toward the allure of the past, following my sense that other artists once occupied this space when they wanted to be alone.

I think about the artists who led public lives but were haunted by private experiences, hovering in a corner over a cigarette; ordinary men suffering a campesino's qualms. I follow the thicket of brush lined with old beer bottles, surveying rickety homes that smell of preserved history, where I can hear the buzz of cars on a distant highway. I come to alleyways like this to linger, collect spirits among the trash, recover the discarded parts of people's lives. In many ways I move inside my Yakima again, here in San Antonio. The wafts of pulled pork and bonfires that linger in the air pull me back into the realities that defined my childhood and still shape me today.

After a while, I return to the steps of the former Salute Bar and to what is now called TBA Bar—a cool, dimly lit hipster hangout with black curtains covering the windows. Inside, the tight space's walls are painted a deep, dark red that bleeds a gothic vibe. I study this interior, which was once congested with conjunto stars and corridistas. I squeeze the spirits from these walls like lemon juice. There, in the corner, might have been the stage that lifted so many greats into stardom. The back of the bar is decorated with Victorian furniture laced in red upholstery and lit up beneath a chandelier. I pause for a moment while episodes of *Seinfeld* stream from a television on mute.

I order a sour beverage cut with cucumber and packed with the punch of salt. I hope that this bar's location might transport me into the past, because I believe in the power of places to reconnect us with history. I believe that if we sit in the places of our elders long enough, we can conjure up the feeling of having a conversation with the past—if not the pasts of others, then at least our own.

I let my mind resound with the accordions that used to make these walls ricochet with conjunto. I try to envision the people who crammed themselves into this place to hear a bit of themselves in the instrument. I think, once more, of the history. How the origin of the accordion in Texas was before the 1900s, predating the dictatorship of Porfirio Díaz and the Mexican Revolution, and as far back as the time of Spanish rule.

Monterrey, the biggest industrial capital of Mexico, is central to the accordion's rise in Texas. The city had looked to Europe for cultural guidance and affirmation, as well as economic assistance. It was the hub of European arts and culture—circuses, concerts, puppet shows, and accordion music—and it was the only place for hundreds of miles where people could get any formal instruction in music. As the center of bourgeoisie life, the city had culture like the Italian opera, which introduced operatic influences like the canción and the bel canto. From Germanic communities, who settled in Mexico as brewmasters in the 1860s, emerged varieties of dance like the polka. Monterrey's prosperous German population may also have introduced the accordion to the area, along with other Polish and Czech settlers who settled San Antonio. The cultural movement that developed in Monterrey eventually diffused into places like neighboring Texas.

Monterrey's proximity to the border and to railroads enabled not just significant cultural exchange, but also enormously lucrative trade and contraband. Railroads through Monterrey provided Texans with crucial sources of material goods from Europe, as well as established European buyers for southern cotton to fund the American Civil War. From these dramas, many corridos emerged, telling stories of tequileros and run-ins with Texas sheriffs.

Corridos originated during the Mexican Revolution, in which music functioned as a form of reportage. Songs recounted the brave tales of revolutionaries fighting to protect indigenous farmers, like the cavalries of Emiliano Zapata. Music also offered a way to beat back government oppression and resist totalitarianism. Elders organized themselves around an ideology of melody, playing and producing their own corridos that educated the communities about the status of the war, increased morale, and demanded change and decolonization of their land. Corridos told of the disparities between rich and poor and rallied people against the dictatorship.

After the war came the Prohibition era. Songs emerged about the adventures of tequileros, who smuggled alcohol into the United States on horseback, and about outlaw country and violent run-ins with Texas rangers. Then corridos evolved into drug ballads, also called narcocorridos, which were dedicated to the violent narratives of cartel wars and bloody territorial disputes, as well as to the drug narratives of the U.S.–Mexico border conflicts. Border ballads shaped the notion of what it meant to be Mexicans abroad. Norteña music embodied the feelings of estrangement that came with being marginalized, displaced, and exploited.

Oppressive working conditions in Mexico and Díaz's slaughter of indigenous communities led to the Mexican Revolution and intensified immigration to Texas, reinforcing norteño culture into the state's already Mexicanized society. The American economic expansion of the 1920s effectively closed off the border and eclipsed Monterrey's influence over Texas. But the accordion's cultural influence had already put down deep roots.

Over time, as laborers moved up from Mexico and into Texas, they absorbed the music of the rich and they made it into their own, creating a tradition as vibrant as the ones in Mexico. Big musical ensembles, which toured and played for the wealthy, were inaccessible to the poor. Instead, salón music and accordion–bajo sexto groups thrived. These ensembles used more affordable instruments, were cheaper to hire since they had no formal training, and were more mobile. They played in pulquerías (taverns) and fiestas, houses and plazas. Musicians often lived in poverty, finding work in the fields and seeking it in cantinas and houses and on street corners. When the community needed to dance, the players would come together spontaneously in makeshift ensembles. They depended on these working-class atmospheres for employment.

Norteño music is rooted in the turbulent and isolated regions of northern Mexico, where indigenous and mestizo heritage communities lived in deserts and rugged mountain regions. In northern Mexico, the Pasitas, Janambres, Yaqui, and other indigenous people were persecuted by the Mexican government. From these regions emerged ballads—which also functioned as musical newspapers— of indigenous heroes and the fierce personalities of figures like peasants, laborers, and the underclass, rustlers, gangsters, border raiders, and bank robbers. For a long time, norteña was rejected as a legitimate art form because of its themes of illegal border crossing and drug trafficking. It wasn't until the 1960s, when the Mexican diaspora became a political force in remittance-dependent Mexico, that corridos as a whole became a beloved national genre. It is music firmly grounded in the contemporary migrant experience, in the ongoing hardships of the Mexican diaspora that involve crossing borders and abandoning family. Until recently, it was even sung in indigenous dialect. Norteña celebrates a distinct working-class culture that is not assimilated to these lands.

Later that evening in San Antonio, I sit at a hipster juice bar to talk with Aaron Salinas, a music instructor at the Conjunto Heritage Taller and member of the indie orquesta latina (Latin orchestra) group Volcán. Everywhere around us there are spurts of renewal, old buildings being restored and rebranded. This is a sensitive subject between those who embrace change and benefit from it and those who are displaced by it. As a young man who represents all that is modern-day San Antonio, Aaron is an unlikely proponent of the conjunto heritage. He is a software engineer passionate about preserving the oral tradition of elders.

"It's important not to let our language, our tradition die," he tells me. "To preserve but also to progress. To teach the traditional way and also incorporate the new."

Aaron has been a student of conjunto since the age of eight, when he discovered his father's accordion in a closet. He battled with the shame associated with the instrument—that it's antiquated, backward, working class, and uncommon. For years, he kept his study of it a secret. But now he senses a resurgence of interest. "People now are starting to grab onto their identity again. They're reconnecting with their roots more than ever."

In terms of what conjunto used to be, a lot of what once defined San Antonio no longer exists, he says. The venues for performing conjunto music are almost gone. The area has a thriving music scene but there's more demand for rock, metal, and pop punk music. In all the cars I ride in, I don't hear a single conjunto accordion beat. Not one radio blasts with the corridos that still thrive in Yakima, Washington. There's a feeling among some locals that conjunto is a thing of the past, of our elders. But Aaron is focused on bringing it all back.

Aaron offers talleres (music classes) with the Guadalupe Cultural Arts Center, where he's focused on developing a holistic curriculum for the community. "A lot of people learn by ear, in the oral tradition. Not in the classical tradition. I'm looking to combine both approaches." To preserve the oral tradition is to recommit to the work of building and honoring our communities. It is to sit on the receiving end of knowledge, embodying rituals that connect us with the past. By offering lessons that speak to both desires—to preserve and to innovate—he hopes to make accordions accessible to a wide audience. To Aaron, there's no sense picking up the accordion without the desire to also learn its history and its roots around the world.

In a city where wealth is displacing so many people, Aaron doesn't want music to be available only to the privileged. He hopes to embrace inclusivity, and to not let pride or traditional ideas get in the way of progress. "Music should be for the people, the working class. [It] should be free, passed on in the way of the past where everyone shares in the music." But, he adds, it's a delicate balance to navigate between the old and new worlds. What conjunto was and what it meant to our parents, we'll never know. "But we have to do our best to play it and find value in our current state."

By the time I leave Aaron and the juice bar, the Tejano blue sky is awash in pink. At the intersection of Josephine and St. Mary's Streets, I sit on a curb next to storm drains big enough to swallow men. Nearby, I can see the turquoise walls of a shuttered salón beneath old-English lettering and Aztec print. I sit in the weakening light, letting my spirit sink with the sunset, waiting for the moment when old ghosts might emerge. These structures are reminders of what will become of all of us. A sudden wind kicks up as the horizon crushes the remaining light. I stand and continue on my path to a club, into an underworld that still thunders with dancing boots.

◆◆◆◆

I wake the following morning and find my way to an old road near Highway 90 where conjunto used to thrive. Now, there's nothing but debris: junkyards and mechanic shops occupy what were once popular conjunto salónes. In this wasteland, I've come to visit the famous Del Bravo Records—Texas's oldest record shop, wedged among the junk.

Entering the shop feels like stepping into the 1960s—a sarcophagus of old sonidos. I trace my fingers over stacks of Tejano, conjunto, norteño, and oldies music, parting stacks of CDs to touch the life preserved in them. Flaco Jiménez, Valerio Longoria, Los Pavos Reales, Toby Torres, Lydia Mendoza—all people that Del Bravo recorded out of a garage studio. Here lie the records of Chalino Sánchez, Los Cadetes de Linares, Ramón Ayala, and other heavyweights who passed through San Antonio and whose voices carried through the fields of my home in Yakima. The cover art often shows images of cowboys leaning against wooden fences between horses and accordions, the men's wild faces set against the landscapes that raised them.

Del Bravo's owner, Rodolfo Gutierrez, sits with me to tell me his history. His family recorded over twenty-five thousand songs, and even took part in composing the famous "Puño de Tierra" that solidified Ramón Ayala as the King of Accordion. Gutierrez's father worked in construction but became a sound technician on the weekends when he recorded musicians out of his rickety garage.

"It was low-budget. The insulation was hanging from the ceiling and my father would staple egg cartons to the walls to soundproof it from the bus stop across the street." To minimize interference, he had to time his recording sessions around the bus schedule. Growing up around the garage, Gutierrez says, he met a lot of musicians. The corridistas would sometimes come to the studio too drunk to remember their own lines.

He shows me a display case that contains Selena paraphernalia and a dress that Lydia Mendoza once performed in. "This is our culture," he says, dusting off the case. "We are a people who cross back and forth between Mexico and Texas, and there's nothing strange about that for us. But we are also aware that we have to act differently. We're still like outsiders on our own land. In the United States we're not 'American enough' and in Mexico we're not 'Mexican enough.'"

At Del Bravo, the aim is to connect people to the past by keeping their heritage alive. "CDs helped us keep our language when we got punished for speaking Spanish in school," Gutierrez says. I tell him that I too was disciplined in school for speaking my language. "But they could never tear down our culture. We relearned our language from our music." He tells me how Tejanos were persecuted on both sides of the border for their multifaceted identities. Del Bravo has even been raided by immigration enforcement. "Our DNA is on both sides of the river," he says. "I'm already home on both sides of the border." To him, living in two places simultaneously is what it means to be Texas–Mexican.

Many musical influences collide in San Antonio, and conjunto has long been in conversations with other genres. Conjunto, Gutierrez says, is not music for the rich. "It's for the person who hurts when his wife has left him," for the working-class man who has been crushed by the tragedies of poverty.

I ask him about the differences between conjunto and norteño. "For Texans, conjunto and norteño are the same thing. It just depends on what side of the border you're on." He tells me that norteño is getting big in San Antonio—the Sinaloan kind, which blasts its banda instruments harder than any conjunto instrument. Sinaloan music is heavy on brass, woodwind, and percussion instruments.

"That's not *my* music," his sister interjects from behind the counter. To her, Texas music is its own unique thing. It depends on who you ask.

Gutierrez tells me about several musicians who blend genres, like Manuel "The Singing Sergeant" Guerrero, a military man who was stationed in San Antonio and Germany. "He played the accordion in Germany and they loved him there. He picked up some German songs and he played them here in San Antonio and they loved him here." Mingo Saldivar is another musician who experimented with merging cultural influences, playing conjunto with a zydeco influence. Linda Ronstadt took the Roy Orbison song "Blue Bayou" and translated it into Spanish, making it her own. There was a commercial incentive to cross genres, but it was also a sign of respect—as Gutierrez put it, "a good musician knows another good musician."

His wife is from Japan and is also a conjunto connoisseur. They met in 1981 at the Conjunto Festival in San Antonio, which includes international acts like the Japanese conjunto band Los Gatos. They sing in Spanish and are very well received by San Antonians, Gutierrez says, "because they are giving tribute to our community. The art form of conjunto started here, but it's going all over the world." Flaco Jiménez did well touring in Japan. Even pachuco homeboy culture, the lowrider subculture of oldies music, exists in Japan. Music travels, moves, merges. And so do we.

I thank Gutierrez for his wisdom and I leave with a handful of CDs. I emerge from the store and am back in San Antonio, ready to bend to the will of this land and its global influences.

◆◆◆◆◆

Later that day, Aaron gives me a ride to the Guadalupe Cultural Arts Center in his beat-up pickup truck. On the drive, we pass many of the vibrant murals that adorn San Antonio. At the Center, we meet several fedora-capped elders—Juan Tejeda, Rudy Lopez, Valeria Alderete—who have mentored Aaron. Under the glare of sunlight breaking through the glass brick of the Center, we gather to discuss the evolution of accordion music in Texas.

"Texas was always and will continue to be indigenous lands," says Juan Tejeda, speaking through a thick nest of beard and mustache. Tejeda is a musician, writer, scholar, and creator of the internationally renowned Tejano Conjunto Festival. He is also former director of the GCAC and a friend of Flaco Jiménez. "In the early 1800s the gringos came and brought their accordions to mestizo and indigenous lands. Then the Mexicanos adopted the accordion in the early 1900s." He describes the mixture of immigrants, the Germanic influences, and the constant wars in Texas that informed the Tejano experience. "Tejas is a prime example of border music—the fusion that took place among our communities.

"Conjunto is original to Texas music," Tejeda continues. "If you don't have an accordion it's not conjunto. It is the only instrument that can capture the intricacies of San Antonian reality." But he also emphasizes that conjunto is *not* norteño music, as the repertoire and the instrumentation are different. Each genre evolved on different sides of the border with unique cultural influences, including one another. Tejanos, he says, are in constant flow to and from Mexico. They exist in two atmospheres, living and thriving on two planes of existence. "To be Tejano is to be *Texas*–Mexican," Mexicans influenced by Texas realities.

Aaron interjects. To him, "there's no answer to what Texas is. Are we of Spanish, indigenous, Germanic, or Mexican origin? That is the question. That is the nature of Texas. A lot of people have been here for generations, since when Texas *was* Mexico . . . It means something different to every person you ask." Texas is proud of this confluence of realities, he says. "But sometimes it leads to an unproductive 'How Mexican, how Texan are you?' debate."

"Tejas is the fusion of global influences," Rudy Lopez adds. "We've integrated many cultures into our accordion, integrated Black traditions like 'The Bolero' by Longoria, Colombian cumbia, blues, and rock and roll."

This circle of elders is a symposium for the future. Conjunto is the soundtrack to their past. There's a consensus that the world is fractured and that young people are in a deep search for something meaningful—and that they're not finding these answers in adults. Music seems to offer one way toward healing, a roadway back to one's roots.

This is also what the accordion has done for me. Corridos bring me back to my past, when I was deeply immersed in campesino worldviews and made promises to save my people.

These elders also share the shame they carried growing up. "We hid ourselves from who we were," Tejeda says. "This school system was and continues to be a very racist system. They don't teach our culture; they make us feel ashamed." To this group, accordion playing is an act of resistance, despite its complicated history and European origins.

Speaking Spanish continues to be a form of resistance in San Antonio. "Texas has tried to abolish our language but we continue to fight to speak our Spanish—even though we also recognize that Spanish is a colonizer language that displaced indigenous communities," Tejeda says. In response to the land's complex history, this group wants to reestablish a way of life that merges and uplifts various identities.

The GCAC's mission is not only to preserve, but to perpetuate culture through formal classes and community events. The cultural programming they offer creates a space for people to express themselves—and, in the eyes of the government, conveys legitimacy. But they can't enact this cultural preservation alone.

"The infrastructure is needed if conjunto is going to survive," Aaron says. As I had already noticed, it isn't very present in the city: conjunto no longer plays on television or on local radio stations, only on obscure internet stations supported by aficionados. The genre is still very grassroots—when major labels pulled out in the 1980s, it was the community that kept conjunto alive—and it thrives best when capitalism doesn't interfere.

But conjunto is not dead in San Antonio—it just needs nurturing. Elsewhere, in communities nearer to the border like the Valley in southern Texas, many young people are picking up the instrument in school, and the genre is thriving. Little by little the infrastructure is growing, the group agrees.

"It's a miracle that conjunto and our people have survived for so long, against the pressure to assimilate, against racism," Tejeda says. "It is a testament to the strength of our people and our hearts. It only gets stronger. We Tejanos unite the old world with the new world, and the world is opening up to us."

After the panel, Aaron and I head to the Dakota, a bar in

another part of town, to meet two conjunto legends: accordionist Benito Medina and bajo sexto player Richard Castillo. These two elders, with slicked-back white hair and wearing green and maroon guayaberas, step onto the stage for a video shoot and play the music of old times. "Bene," as they call him, has been inducted into three halls of fame. He cradles his deep-sea-blue accordion that gleams with diamonds like dragon skin—a three-row Hohner Gabbanelli model. His fingers press the pearl buttons, typing patterns into his chest and tearing sounds from the reeds that slice the air like razor blades. Richard's bajo sexto was famously made in the indigenous Purépecha land of Paracho, Michoacán. He plays beautifully, casting big shadows as a backdrop for the accordion to shine against. After a couple of songs, Bene switches out accordions for another Hohner model—a gray one with a sharper sound.

A few songs later, Aaron steps onto the stage with his accordion to join them, adding his own color with a pink guayabera. His fingers are fresh and strong and flash rhythms at lightning speed, playing old tunes that are rarely featured by contemporary conjunto musicians. His right hand does most of the work because conjunto relinquishes the left bass side to the bajo sexto.

After a couple of video shoots, we sit together over food. I am in the presence of many accumulated years of experience.

Bene used to work as an electrician who serviced telephone poles. "I never toured because I didn't want to sign a contract with no one," he says. He doesn't regret never having toured, because many of the accordionists who did died with nothing, living out their last days in homeless shelters. "Back then," he tells me, "people would sign contracts with an X, because they were illiterate." Musicians were often taken advantage of by record companies.

He and Richard reminisce about the good old days in the conjunto salónes like the East Side Club, Rainbow Club, Las Vegas Club, El Flamingo, and Lerma's Night Club. These were all places where they went to find community, healing, love. They agree that clubs today aren't as vibrant as they were in the sixties. We talk about the struggle to preserve salónes and how people used to play music for free, as a communal expression of love.

"It's not about community anymore," Aaron adds. "It's now about 'how much can we get paid?'"

I think about the struggling musicians Bene mentioned. Though they played for love and community, they also lived hard lives without compensation or reward. These were traveling musicians like my grandfather. Ideally, there's a middle ground where musicians can have both community support and an opportunity to make a good living.

At the end of the meal, Bene autographs his CDs for me. "People miss this music," he says.

They also miss the sacred weekend rituals that conjunto made possible.

"People labored during the week because they knew Saturday was coming," Rudy Lopez says, leaning in. People who labored picking cotton, cacahuates (peanuts), strawberries. "We would drive around for miles, following that conjunto sound, looking for that next conjunto gathering."

Before we break up and say our goodbyes, Rudy comes up close to me and says, "We'll see each other again—'rodando se encuentran las piedras.'" It's a tough expression to translate. Roughly, it means that you should not do others wrong, because along the way, you will cross paths again, and that out there, tumbling away in our human journey, we will also find ourselves.

◆◆◆◆◆

That evening I meet with Gary Smith, owner of the historic Alamo Music Center—ground zero for selling instruments to many conjunto legends.

"The 1960s was lively, vibrant," Smith tells me. "We had

Narciso Martínez and Santiago—each equally credited with the invention of accordion conjunto. They were everywhere."

Despite the instrument's popularity during that decade, he says, in the 1970s the accordion became a joke. It didn't become cool again until the 1990s. "New musicians [were] picking it up and displaying their prowess with the accordion. Flaco Jiménez toured with the Rolling Stones," he adds emphatically. Jiménez collaborated with the Rolling Stones on their *Voodoo Lounge* album.

Today, he sees the accordion as very much alive. "Nowadays, with folk and Americana, if you don't have an accordion, you're considered a loser. I'm now selling accordions to schools because accordions are being taught [there]," a sign that Tejano music is "here to stay." Like others I've spoken to, he also sees the instrument as a valuable method of cultural preservation. For people who want to learn the accordion, he advises that they find an instructor to learn in the tradition of the old days.

I ask him how accordions fit into the state of the world today, and he takes a moment to consider the question.

"Music is the only cure for the fragmentation in our world," he says. "Music is the universal language and people can appreciate the complexity [of life] if they just stop and listen." In a world grown loud with conflict and political differences, he believes the accordion is teaching us to hear and to dance again. He sees conjunto and Texas as synonymous. "How people act and react to that music is magic. The joy that it brings, how it moves people to congregate year after year. It's like the Woodstock Festival here."

I ask him where exactly all these conjunto accordionists are, since I'm having trouble finding any on my trip.

"Right now, they're at work, they're at school." They're living out their lives as any conjunto artist does. The accordion is still rooted in the working class. The conjunto musician is still laboring away in the world, consumed with eking out a living as best he can. I know that it can't be an easy balance to strike. I am against the silence, against so much work, if it means it drowns out our ability to celebrate life.

—♦♦♦♦—

The San Antonio day grows dim. Cicadas chirp hard in the dying evening. Their wings vibrate like accordion reeds, reminding me of the beauty of sounds and our imperative to protect them. Here at the Judson Nature Trails, my final stop in the city, I try to hold all the knowledge that has been shared with me by people who have seen and experienced a different world than mine.

I think about how Aaron has shown me that conjunto music is full and alive and thriving in San Antonio. He demonstrates a vigor for living through his art and his teaching, giving me hope for its future. I see the welcoming nature of his community, how the people within it embrace one another, uplift one another, empower one another. How the music offers them a safe place in which to exist.

I value the work that Aaron does with his elders, working hard to develop a common language of music between the generations. He studies the work of his ancestors and preserves it while also incorporating his own. In doing so, he also inches closer to finding a possible solution for the younger folk who are trying to find themselves.

Our instruments have a vital importance in our communities. They represent ways to preserve history, culture, and language. They are also sources of spiritual power. To hold an accordion is to orient a person's heart in that direction at any given moment. We all are brothers and sisters regardless of what attracted us to this instrument.

LAS AFUERAS

(Norteño: An Ideology of Melody)

ALL MY LIFE, I BURIED MYSELF IN CORRIDOS' SOUNDS OF SORROW. I sat in parks and at backyard barbecues, absorbing the collective rage of my people and their urge to return home at whatever cost. I listened while my elders painted pictures of what it was like to live in Mexico, hoping they would draw me road maps to a better life. But that life, for me, would never be in Mexico. In many ways, my family is still firmly lodged in an experience I can no longer lay claim to. I buried myself in falsehoods, in worlds and ideas that existed for them but not for me. I was stuck longing for something that was lost to me from the beginning. And that longing kept me from learning to make a home in Yakima, and from making a home inside myself.

All my life, I've done what my family has asked me to and unmoored myself from the idea of Yakima's landscapes, but now they must understand that I suffer a new loneliness, without the ability to communicate it to them. To do so would introduce a new level of hurt into their narrative, which I cannot do to them. Every bit of our story that I discard—the legacy of repression and silence—is that much more I relinquish of my family. That much more pain that I gather into music and writing.

I still think fondly about how my corridista heritage began in the belting and wailing rituals of my elders in Yakima while I was still in my mother's stomach. This heritage continued in the emotional uproar of music in backyard gatherings, an opportunity for my people to release everything they had bottled up. I think about how I was raised around relatives who cried only under the curative ceremonies of corridos. People who contended with the harsh realities of El Norte through songs that documented the traumas along the journey from Mexico to Yakima.

I recognize myself in the straining voices of cowboy corridistas like Chalino Sánchez, the prolific word- and song-smith of the gunslinging underworld. Through singers like him, I understood the struggles of fierce men and women who endured in silence for their children and for their future. I knew of fierce desert lands that boiled our blood and sedated our spirits during picking seasons. I knew of fires that ravaged our hills, of fiestas that put fire to our feet. The arrogance of Chalino's words, the posturing of his lyrics, his delivery in that fiery Sinaloan dialect—all these things brought attention to the violence that was happening to campesinos. He protested poverty and he survived the people's hardship.

But corridos could also make strong men crumble. For that reason, I also feared them. I feared their ability to one day come for me, foretelling the grand fall that inevitably comes for us all.

In my adulthood, corridos are giving me back the framework

for understanding my suffering on a much larger, collective level. They are helping me recognize that much of my suffering has been inherited; a deep-rooted generational trauma that I had no control over. Their words gave birth to people like me even before I understood them.

Now, I come full circle by writing my own songs. Like the corridistas I grew up hearing, I sit around firepits and grills to talk of the painful and violent things my father couldn't express. Through songs, I try to have hard conversations with myself about what it means to be a man, how I can express my emotions without feeling shame or without their swallowing me whole. As I try to appeal to this idea of a grandfather and to ancestral ghosts, to this notion of myself as a mentor for my son, music gives me some sense of control. With corridos I delve deep into the marrow of our human story. I return to the words I never could speak as a child, ready now to belt them out in song.

I think about how my father guarded his wounds from those around him. He lived in quiet torment, modeling restraint when so many others around me seemed to embrace emotional release. This kept him at a remove from his family. It also taught me to act the way he did: I learned to hold back my feelings by observing him. I learned to swallow my words. And so, as a boy, my father guarded me from many of the family blood ballads—stories that his father was abusive, that his brother was murdered, that his mother's death was suspicious, that the Mexican homeland was a place of war and feuding families with conflicts that spilled over into Yakima.

I think about the conditions that might lead a father to remove himself from his family; if that is ever a compassionate decision that comes from recognizing his own flaws and knowing they're incurable. It is possible that this assumption credits my grandfather with too much. To be a true man is to continue on with a family, even knowing what lives inside you.

My people have developed so many forms of resistance to keep from crumbling into the ground they harvest. They have maintained their autonomy through music, songs that speak the truth about the migrant's life, the breakup of families, the racial conflicts of the border. I sit with the words of men in poverty who sang of our superhuman quality to subvert oppression on two fronts—from the South and from the North. I sit with the tremors of corridos that escape from passing cars and lowriders, giving us power and asserting our humanity when people refuse to see us.

I see the new face of the mojados, of bandits and revolutionaries cruising the streets of Yakima and across the nation, trying to imagine themselves out of poverty and searching for role models to teach them how to exist in this divided town. They ride like the revolutionaries, seeing themselves as the border raiders of today, reclaiming land and resisting assimilation. They search as I did for a place to call home, as defiant as the ballad tradition always was.

I pass my accordion around from hand to hand, from sorrow to sorrow, soaking it in the agonies of others. I surrender the accordion to those whose spirits I want to merge with mine. I lend the accordion to my father before leaving Yakima for Seattle, so that he may work through his pain and find healing. I offer up the accordion as a way to refocus his mind on something good. I remind him to keep up the practice, to keep those keys warm, his rhythms raw. I tell him not to neglect the instrument, not to turn away from its magic, because to put it aside is to let it die—to let something inside you perish.

"The reeds need constant airflow or you'll suffocate the sound," I tell him. It is an instrument to save you from the brink of darkness.

I feel a familiar pressure in my stomach when I come at my history alone, digging into my grandfather's story when everyone else in my family has seemingly moved on. I know there's no logic in pursuing dead stories, and I want to take comfort in what people tell me about my grandfather.

But the more they say, and the more I pursue him, the less I feel I truly know about him. There is only one way to find the answer. I must embark on travels that engage all my senses, experiencing for myself the sights, sounds, and smells of Mexico's ancient landscapes.

BRIDGE

WITH MY EYES OPEN

(Mexico)

IT'S BEEN YEARS SINCE I VISITED MEXICO, YEARS SINCE I HOPPED into a taxi in the early dark hours to watch with hazy eyes as the industrial zones of Guadalajara flowed past me. It's been years since I was this on edge, choked by the smog of Mexico's industrial cities and by the unease that comes from lands that grow stranger to me with each visit. My feelings for this place hover somewhere between love and hate for the things I mostly no longer know: the grand plazas, bustling night markets, street music—all of which keep these lands rich with family traditions.

I'm on my way to the bus terminal destined for Michoacán, where my cousin will pick me up. I can't help but feel like I am lying to myself. I have come to Mexico to pursue fragments of a distant story. At times, I worry that I'm living out a delusion, thinking I could make sense of the ghosts that have haunted our family. In chasing my grandfather's story, I may be reawakening a chapter of our history that may hurt others, or insult the hard work they've done to trap this demon. I fear I may be giving too much energy to a man who dedicated none of his to my father's life or to mine.

There are certain roads we are not meant to take. Spirits linger on those roads, threatening to expose us to things that we cannot come back from. The journey to access my parents' stories is full of such dark and dangerous roads. I channel all these worries, all this sensation, into my accordion, and I come to Mexico with an open heart.

⬥⬥⬥⬥⬥

Arriving in Mexico is a drop shock—the ice-cold realization that life operates differently here and that I must adapt quickly. Its landscapes draw a different persona out from me; a version of myself I might have known had I been born here. I have just left the baroque city of Morelia, which took me on a journey through seventeenth-century history. It is the capital of Michoacán, the place where all buses must pass through before fanning out into the enigmatic outskirts of mountainscapes and villages.

Now, I am in a car on a country highway with my uncle, whom I call my cousin. He is the only person who can lead me safely through Mexico. In our family lineage, his roots in the country go deepest. This younger uncle of mine is my key to reaching my ancestral homelands and finding the truth hidden behind the front lines of warring territories.

Out here in the expanse between Morelia and Tacámbaro, I bathe in the honeyed sunlight, feeling as if the majestic landscape is transcribing stories onto my skin.

I think about all the stories I'd share with my ancestors in

Mexico if I could. I think of the tragedies I would impart to them in the form of corridos, telling them what it's been like in El Norte. Finally, now that I'm here, I will embrace the true power of the form I took for granted growing up.

Suddenly, the car's axle breaks and we spin out of our lane. My cousin fights the steering wheel for control and is unable to brake. We veer in and out of oncoming traffic in what seems like slow motion. I feel nothing until the car dips over the edge of the road and my cousin, giving the wheel one last yank, finally yells that he's lost control.

"Agárrate, Noé!" His words are hard, guttural, telling me to hold on.

We slam into a bank lined with big rocks, and the impact sends the vehicle somersaulting. In a rapid flow of spinning images—darkness, brightness, darkness, brightness—we tumble over cactus and toward the realm of my ancestors. We can do nothing but hold onto our flesh, revealed in this instant as a false idea of ourselves. I shut and open my eyes at different moments as we tumble and toss, my mind somehow both suspended and intact. Between snapshots of the landscape and the deafening impacts of the car against the ground, I glimpse the final image: a fast-approaching tree. Out of instinct, I curl up into a ball and close my eyes, unwilling to die with my eyes open.

Darkness.

When I will my eyes to open again, they are greeted by an inverse world. I'm choked by the smell of gas. A faint voice orients me back to my body.

"¿Estás bien, Noé?" My cousin is struggling to pull himself free and is yelling at me to get out quickly. "¡Salte rápido!"

It takes me a moment to realize where I am: hanging upside down from my seat belt like a drying piece of meat. We fight to free ourselves. My cousin drops onto a bed of glass and slithers through a narrow opening of light.

"Get out quick," he says, coughing through the smoke. I am still struggling to unclip myself. Finally, I drop from my suspension and pull myself over glass and through an opening. I feel a heavy pain in my ribs.

In a daze I grip my ribs with bloodied hands, beholden again to this flesh that no longer feels like mine. It feels like my body is only half risen, forcibly thrust into a space between life and death. I walk away from the rubble, my vision refracted a million ways by the shattered glass. It's clear now that I need to prepare myself for all the things I must do before death. I must make pacts with the spirits and the demons now.

Pedestrians and heavily armed police rush to the scene. Before they reach us, I dive back into the cockpit of the car, into the smell of gas and the gush of oil, and I crawl around in search of my accordion.

But there's no sign of it. Some rabbits pass by the wreckage and I crawl back out.

"Move away from the car," officers order me from a distance.

I ignore them and I search the back of the car. To my relief, the accordion is in the trunk, where I'd forgotten I put it. It falls to the ground and I grab it before I am pulled away.

"¿Hay heridos?" An officer asks if we are injured. "¿Necesitan ambulancia?" People come at us from all sides offering assistance. An officer looks me up and down suspiciously. I have a certain look about me and my passport confirms it: American.

"Do you want an ambulance?" officers repeat to me in my daze. I tell him no when I want to tell him yes; that the land has devoured a precious part of me. All I want is to stay transfixed on the beauty of this landscape. Can he save me from being swallowed whole by it?

I take a moment to rest among the rocks. There is a sharp pain in my ribs and I am too afraid to look inside my shirt and inspect my chest. I fear what might spill out. I fear I will not have the strength to piece myself together again. More hares dart for cover nearby. I keep my accordion case closed. I'm not ready to look in that case either, or deprive myself of the hope that what's left inside is still special and intact.

As the whirl of the event dies down, I watch a tow truck back into the bank and roll the wreckage over to reveal the extent of the damage. After reeling the car onto the truck's bed, the driver takes a moment to reflect.

"El Diablo no duerme," he says to us. The devil doesn't sleep. Yet another rabbit darts past me.

I must learn to vanquish the delusion of permanence and accept that this body, and what emerges from it, is only temporary—even the words I'm writing now. I must withdraw and emerge as the desert wildflowers do, making room for others to take their place in this world. I must surrender the idea that whatever I dream up is the only reality and that my concerns are all that matter. I must believe that pain and suffering are not permanent, even though they are constant.

We ride with the tow truck driver into town, where the worms sleep in mezcal elixirs and monarch butterflies console the living for Día de Los Muertos. The lands here are harsh at every turn, the sinkholes and cliffsides a reminder that the country is after you always. I kiss my dream-catcher necklace to keep my spirit close to me.

WHERE DREAMS LEAVE OFF
(Tacámbaro)

TACÁMBARO IS A VILLAGE ON THE OUTSKIRTS OF CONFLICT. IT IS AN indigenous Purépecha city where my cousin and his family reside. There, we lie low while we figure out how to locate the source of my family's pain. I settle into the three-story structure where my cousins live, a bare-bones house stacked into the high hills. The shared housing is made of cement and plastered with the narratives of many passing tenants. Many families of laborers come here to rest between their shifts. One person will leave his dreams to go to work, and another person will take his place, drop down dead tired, and pick up where the first dream left off. These gentle folk have kindly taken me in. They show me to a blue room on the second floor, where I too will merge my dreams with those of the laborers.

I rest my sore bones under a single light bulb, under caving walls that are blackened by mold and lined with exposed circuitry. Never have I been so tired. I move my fingers over my accordion case, which rests on my bed beside me. I try not to think about what the crash has done to the instrument, to my ribs, to my feelings about not having been born in Mexico. I cannot shake the feeling that Mexico and the United States cannot both exist within me. Striking an allegiance with the middle ground would possibly mean depriving myself of both worlds.

I sink into a slow slumber, while the city of Tacámbaro resounds with nightlife. Kids kick rocks beneath my bedroom window while their mothers and grandmothers watch them from a distance. Accordions shake the mountains as banda blasts from cars. Someone clips their toenails to the sound of singing crickets, dogs bark from distant rooftops, and beer bottles roll over cement.

To this soundtrack I try to slither into sleep. I think back to years ago, sometime in college, when my cousin and I first met—two relatives living distant lives. I was staying with him in Morelia, at a boarding school for indigenous students called La "Che" (named for Che Guevara), when the dorms went up in riot. Students barricaded themselves into different corners of the courtyard, beating back swelling waves of violence. They were in uproar, launching rocks, bottles of glass, and other projectiles at one another. One youth stumbled back in from the street, half-conscious and blinded by his own blood.

"Don't go outside," my cousin insisted. In an effort to keep the peace, he rushed to quell and de-escalate the violence, shouting at people to disperse or else they'd have to deal with him. No one dared. I saw him handling the chaos with ease. For whatever reason, people feared him.

"The students govern themselves," he told me. "This is the way of our government here." It is the way of these poorly funded school systems, where beds are bunked nine levels high, sandwiching about twenty students and their dreams into a small room, where they must divide all goods and supplies among themselves. Here there are students of dentistry, law, engineering. They have meetings, they assign one another duties, and they take communal responsibility for the success of the whole organization. They take shifts in the kitchen, cleaning out ammonia-stinking bathrooms, keeping accountable to one another. Naturally tensions rise, feuds build. Conflicts like these occur more often than they should.

Come the next morning, everything was business as usual. Students trickled in and out for classes. Some of them were bruised and beaten but no one was yet defeated. Life must go on here, however much harder it falls on those who live it.

While reliving these memories, I let go of consciousness on the bed in Tacámbaro. A plume of firework smoke drifts up from under my window, lit by children. I keep hold of my beaten rib cage.

◆◆◆◆

I wake the next morning to a knock on my bedroom door. My cousin slips into my room and halfway into my dream, wishes me good morning, then hands me his phone—an urgent text from my dad that's made its way down the vine to him and now to me.

"Tell Noé not to go to Colima." My mother's city—only a few hours from where I currently am. "They murdered his uncle, Jorge."

The news sends me into the sensations of another tumbling car crash. My mother's brother—killed the same day I survived the accident. My god, his beautiful face, taken from me for good.

I hold this man in my mind again, this man who I came to love so much in Yakima. He was full of loving enthusiasm for the future of his people, a man who made me believe that we were going to be okay so long as he was in our lives, who always had the time to take our family crabbing in the Puget Sound. For decades he had struggled with his mental health, living the life of a wanderer, in search of whatever fix could take his pain away. Now, he had left us.

━◆◆◆◆◆━

For the first time in years, I go to sit inside a cathedral, in el centro of Tacámbaro, not to pray, really, but to sit safely apart from the world outside and focus on the swirl of pain within. I need to be in a space all on my own, in an atmosphere of frankincense, away from all the eyes fixated on my hurt.

Inside this stone building, I search for the breath that my uncle's death has taken from my family. The loss crushes in on my ribs, making it harder to breathe. Every inhale presses further into my heart. Once again, I begin to feel something like hatred for these lands, for all the family it has violently taken from me: my father's brother, a grandmother, a godfather, and now this most beautiful spirit of an uncle. I loathe this land for all of the stories it has robbed from me. I grow weary under a spell that will not break.

I dip my fingers into the holy water I've restrained myself from touching all these years. It submerges me in a memory, back when I was with my uncle as a boy leaning over the Puget Sound sea, watching the water's murk glistening in the moonlight. I lie on my stomach over wet boards as the pier gently oscillates underneath me. My hands explore this vast water world and tickle the sea awake, playing silent tunes for the fish to entice them closer. I offer them my flesh, beckon them to nibble and hook themselves onto my fingertips. I surrender my hand to the holy water in exchange for a moment with my uncle, for the beauty that once was our family. But the fish no longer come.

I dig deep into the water, try to pull repressed memories and sensations from the sea inside me, to guide me through adulthood's troubled waters. I try to shake hands again with my relatives, with the people who have seen this life before. Life feels empty without them and their guidance. But I stare at these waters and see only myself. The face of the only person who can save me. I am thankful for the loved ones who carried me for as long as they did, but I must craft my own stories now.

I no longer hold my uncle's magic or his loving heart. I no longer carry the flesh of the boy filled with dreams. I am older, wearied by the stories of violence and the many tragedies I've lived through, and the fish can smell it in my hands. Still, I try to anchor myself to that pier. To the past.

When I begin to pull away, an image arises from my memory of the deep sea. It reaches out to me and I pull back. But my uncle emerges to sit on the pier next to me.

"Hola, mijo."

I choke.

"¿Que haces por aquí?" my uncle asks. "What are you still chasing? This is no place for you here anymore. Your peace is elsewhere."

Whatever it is that spared me, whatever I used up that day of the crash while my uncle was being gunned down, I can't help but feel as though I have robbed it from him. If I hadn't come to Mexico that very day, maybe, just maybe, the winds would have saved him instead.

Inside the cathedral I cross my arms on the bench in front of me and dig my face into them to cry. I let my tears run down my cheeks and over the bandana I've fashioned into a face mask. From my eyes, I bring down rain on these lands.

I will carry my uncle inside my accordion now. I vow to carry him in my music.

I sit a bit longer inside my forearms, in the presence of passing villagers. Each person takes their turn at the foot of a shrine to say their prayers in silence. Some of them chant, singing familiar verses. After a few moments, I step back out into the world feeling a little bit lighter, ready to move like a shadow among shadows. To pass the days in silent mourning as I become part of Mexico's narrative once more.

><<<<

How might I still belong on this foreign land? How can I still belong in my own divided body and spirit, which lay claim to both U.S. and Mexican traditions? I peruse the butcher markets that string up animal innards like laundry, I canvass the town square fortified with police and military-grade artillery, and I tiptoe around elderly people on street corners selling whatever goods they can. I want to belong, but somehow, I can't. In response, I hold onto an idea of Mexico, the stories I feel emerging from these landscapes. Mexico to me is only a feeling now.

I come at this city from atop a hill to overlook this mountainous region of avocados and acabados—at the wasted bodies and wearied stories. I come at it from beneath, in the trash that piles on the streets, among the cats that stalk the city perimeters. I am everywhere and nowhere here. Perhaps I am only a spirit that emerged from the rubble of the crash.

Still, because I'm so close to finding answers, I must stay committed to visiting my grandpa's place before I return to my mother in Yakima to comfort her. I need to challenge the mentality that things cannot be altered in our family. I must see the source of hurt for myself, move deeper into the land of my people's origins and change this painful story, especially now that my accordion and I have survived.

Amid so much destruction, I begin to see for myself some of the things that my family exchanged for a different life in El Norte. The pain that they traded for another pain, dying torturously slowly in the United States instead of dying quickly in Mexico.

I have come to Mexico with the mission of seeing my grandfather, but I also feel myself being pulled in so many other directions. The harder I search, the more lost I get. Just like all those who have come before me in my family lineage. People who embarked on a migration in desperation, after some tragedy pushed them to move away. People who could never find a home to replace the homeland they left.

I'm on a journey that clashes with the plans Mexico has for me, it seems. Plans that have long been set in motion by ancestors who could not break their spell. I'm not sure why I thought I could be the one to break it. But we try, generation after generation, to live a lovelier life and come to a softer, less violent end. My presence has disrupted my parents' work to free me from their lands of Tierra Calientes. They wished me free of this place, and now I have returned to it.

Using a cell phone is a solitary act, so I step into a phone booth inside a busy meat market, in the manner that relatives made calls to us from Mexico, to call my mother. Here, the act becomes communal as I muffle my tears to tell her I love her and that I'm sorry I'm not with her right now and sorry that I cannot tell her exactly where I am. I withhold the news about my accident until later. I tell her that I will hold her in my arms when I return and urge her not to come to Mexico for her brother's funeral, because things are really bad and unsafe right now.

I hang up and exit the phone booth under the hard gaze of

armed guards and cowboys in the city square. I walk back to my tenement below the hill, determined still to visit the even more tumultuous lands of my grandfather. For days, I stare from my bedroom window at a black silo of water on a neighbor's rooftop, listening to the sounds of corridos playing from a distant radio.

I find comfort in the wisdom of corridos, in their take on suffering. They teach us that suffering is a part of us, but it doesn't have to destroy us. We can find liberty in embracing our hardships. I think of all the pain still ahead in our lives and the strength I will always find to rise out of the turbulence and flower. I turn my face directly toward the hardships and let them roll over me, surrendering my body to the songs of los corridos.

Here on these lands, I must learn to eulogize not only the past, but the present—actively mourning the things that are dying before my very eyes. Somehow, I have to find a way to describe the agonizing moments of loss, to honor the fading things in my life with words and with songs.

I sit with the members of this household over good meals—frijoles de la hoya with tortilla and avocado. To me, people appear most vulnerable when they eat, sunk like sad animals over their meals. I sit with women who are taco vendors and an avocado farmer with missing front teeth. His straw hat droops to one side, his pants are stained from work, and his feet are calloused and hardened inside cowhide chanclas. My cousin sits to my right, telling tales. His two children are playing and hopping around. His wife and her family speak of other times, older times, when things around here weren't so bad.

They talk of the farm, of all the bugs—the "matacaballos" bug that kills horses, the bees that attack only the eyes, and the wasps that live underground and are unrelenting in their attack against man. They give each other side glances, as if afraid of being overheard, as they talk about the war in Aquila, near where my grandfather lives, and where we'll be heading in a few days.

The war has been long between the people, the cartel, and the government. I don't ask questions. Not today. Today I sit in the comfort of these generous people—distant relatives who have given me a good place to sleep, eat, and to evade suspicion by living in what are essentially indigenous safe houses. Today, I do not want to hear about all the many ways that a man like me can die in Mexico.

They worry about my cousin's plans to take me into the beast of Tierra Caliente, and they exchange concerns in their indigenous tongues. Because of me, he risks his life, I'm aware of this. I've given him multiple opportunities to say no. But he wants this for me; he believes in bringing me some closure. Besides, without him these places are inaccessible to me. There would be no chance of ever penetrating my grandfather's land.

Over café de la hoya, my cousin stretches out his forearm onto the table.

"Mi 'apá, cuando le pica un alacrán, se muere el alacrán." With his other hand he simulates a dying scorpion. He asserts that he has witnessed his father's words come to life about how scorpions die when they sting him. He once watched a scorpion sting his father and then crawl a few feet away to die in agony.

Why this happens, no one knows, he tells me. I imagine his father flexing toxins back into the scorpion, sending a rush of indigenous blood back into the creature, giving it the equivalent of a heart attack. Must be something in his blood, this uncle of mine. Nowadays, his blood is weaker; he lives in the Yakima Valley and is on regular dialysis.

I think of these stories and hold them close. There is some unknown magic inside us all. A power so great it might make us impervious to danger. A similar power saved my life many years ago when I stepped barefoot onto a scorpion.

"No te hizo," my mother would always tell me. As in "it didn't take." I beat the poison naturally.

I'd like to think that I too have the power to keep danger at a distance. These are the kinds of thoughts that I need to have in order to keep going.

––––

Sometimes it takes a frigid Mexican shower to really feel certain things. A bitter cold as frigid as a raging river in the morning. With no water heater in the house, it's the kind of shower that rips the heart out of you. The water smacks me up like spitfire and I think of the AK-47 that an assassin used to gun down my uncle in front of his house in Colima. A high-powered rifle called "cuerno de chivo," Spanish slang for *horn of a goat*. I think of my mother's grief, as violent as the repeated headbutts of a goat ramming into her chest. I step out to dry myself off. When your body experiences the ruthless shock of the cold, it's forced to generate a new kind of warmth. I wait for that sensation to bring the blood back to my veins.

I get dressed and walk downstairs to meet up with my cousin on the front steps. We drink instant coffee and eat pan dulce next to potted roses, watching the smoke rise with the sun. The old ladies have put out their caged parrots to bathe and sing again.

My cousin is a sharp dresser. Long-sleeved button-up shirt, creased pants, polished shoes. He is a student of law. His wife is in nursing. This morning, he makes arrangements on his cell phone for my visit to his birthland.

"Are the roads okay?" I hear him ask. "Prepare two beds and some good camarones," he says. "Traigo un primo, no lo conoces, de los Estados Unidos." *I'm bringing a cousin, you don't know him, he's from the United States.*

He assures me that the roads will be clear, hopefully unlike my last visit to Morelia years ago, when the entire city was caged in by burning buses ignited by cartel–government wars. The city was on lockdown and we couldn't leave.

"Llegaste en la época de los putasos," he says about that last time in Morelia. *You arrived in the era of heavy confrontation.*

There are tribes and there are rules, he says, about the lands we hope to enter, though he's not particularly open about exactly what that looks like. But he looks at my face.

"They'll ask you about that," he says with a nod.

My facial hair. It stinks of Spanish conquistador, unlike his face, which is clean. He doesn't say more. But that's why I have him, to be my passport into a territory that breaks out into civil war on a regular basis. He shifts when I press him about military activity, or the indigenous uprising. I pull back. These are his lands, his people, family he's responsible for. Some things he guards from me, and that is his right. A car crash does not yet make us blood brothers. Ours is a relationship still in progress.

He walks up the steps, still talking on his cell phone, to continue the business of selling his car for scraps. A car he ideally hopes to restore because "no hay de otra." There are no other options in a country like this one, where things must be repaired past their life span. The cars have lived multiple lives and they continue claiming the lives of others.

"The roads are closed," he says. "Too dangerous." We wait.

———

That day I decide to walk off my pain, going up the hill again into Tacámbaro's crowded city square. I move with the people into street markets and meet with a yerbero herbalist elder. I ask her if she has anything for revitalization—for the sadness we sometimes hold.

"Doce flores" and "siete azahares," she says. Two herbal mixtures, teas for the nerves and disturbed dreams. They are meant to restore the energies missing from one's life. Served for people who are "sick in the heart," she says, aiding drinkers in their journey into the dreamworld.

"Here," she says, giving me something else in addition. "It's for all the lurking scorpions and snakes." For all of the venomous things that might lurk around me. May it also help me on my journey, she says, noting I have a shaky spirit. Before I thank her, I also take a handful of copal. For protection.

LA JUGADA

IN TACÁMBARO, THE NIGHT IS HARD AND HEAVY. I AM RESTING ON MY bed upstairs. My cousin is on standby for the call to tell him whether the gunfights have cleared and the conflicts have subsided enough for us to slip past. It has been three nights of worry. Three nights of turning over worst-case scenarios. My heart beats in a countdown. The plan is to move into the war zones of Tierra Caliente under the cover of darkness; a place where at least three cartel organizations, military, and paramilitary clash for power.

"Time to go," my cousin calls. His voice carries up to my room like roasted chiles, rich and wafting.

I rush to pack for the trip into the hot lands of Aquila. I make a quick call to the mother of my baby, saying goodbye to her in the only corner of the room that gets cell reception. I pack the essentials, throw my heavy bag onto my shoulders, and fumble over a few things, including the nugget of copal the herbalist gave me for luck. We will have to get past the checkpoints and the interrogations by heavily armed men. In a region rife with abductions and massacres, we will have to surrender the very idea that we hold rights to our bodies.

We walk down steep steps to a darker road, hoping to wave down a taxi that never seems to come. My blood beats coarsely through me.

"The people in the village are going to question you about some things," my cousin informs me. "Best you get your story straight." His brother waits alongside us. He will be coming along on this journey.

When the taxi finally shows up, I place my accordion into the trunk, trying to conceal the tremors in my hands. There's no turning back now. I am questioning my commitment to the old man; questioning my reasons for unearthing a story that just might not want to be told. I hop into the back seat and hold my backpack like a makeshift airbag. My cousin sits in front. I search desperately for seat belts. I dig my hands into the upholstery. There has to be a seatbelt. I tug and tug at where it should be and all I fish out are images of my car crash.

I haven't had the time to process the experience—I've been too busy trying to keep moving so that my body might forget. This goddamn place. I am distressed by how comfortably people sit close to death here. But then again, here I am. I restrain my hands and push down the idea that tries to swell up inside of me: that all this dreaming, all this hoping and conjuring up old spirits, has actually laid a trap for me. Trickster ghosts have ensnared me into something sinister. We slip quickly into the night and transfer from the taxi onto a chicken bus where I wrestle my accordion onto my lap. I bring into my grandfather's land not just any accordion, but the best-made accordion the world has ever seen. I hope to give it even a moment in his hands.

This land of Tierra Caliente, where my grandfather lives, is a region accosted on three sides by mighty states: Guerrero, the state of Mexico, and Michoacán. It sits in the center of hot, arid lands that offer coastal access to Colombian drug routes and spark brutal fighting over the area's rich resources.

The bus passes through a number of villages. I watch them glow in faint light that reveals cinder-block shacks and impoverished structures. I cling to what feels like a premonition, a sensation in my stomach telling me that I shouldn't go through with this. Under the momentary explosion of light from street lamps, I try to write my thoughts into the crevices of my palm, words like: *I am going into battle with an accordion for a gun.* I aim to defend myself with the guise of a musician. It is my marker of peace and good relations. I have to believe that what I'm doing is the right thing. That I don't come into my grandfather's lands to bring further harm. I press words into my skin to try to turn them into reality.

I hold my accordion case tightly. I still haven't inspected its contents since the car crash.

―――

They emerged from the hills in the middle of the night, when I was dead asleep on a long trip through wild country.

"Los comunitarios," my cousin tells me. An assassin's assassin. Armed members of the community ready for war against narco traffickers. "They're trying to bring back the peace, tearing up roads and setting up curfews." The guerrilla group had slipped past me while my head was cocked back in sleep with arterial veins exposed, at the mercy of this land. AK-47s had swept the bus for enemies and enemy dreams.

I wake in the town of Coalcomán, a mill town of maderos (lumberjacks). Not a soul around. All exits are closed. No one gets out until the fighting has stopped. There are no more drivers available to take us deeper into bush country. Taxis are strictly prohibited from entering conflict zones. But with luck, and the pull my cousin has in the community, we manage to get a ride with a very nervous taxi driver who helps us slip through fog and into the red zones of a regional conflict.

He tears through the streets, his eyes twitching with vigilance. But the drive is smooth and no one interrupts us. Eventually, the taxi man relaxes and can manage better conversation. He begins to air his people's grievances as he tailgates illegal mining trucks, swerving around rock falls and eroded sections of road on dangerous cliffsides.

"The people want liberty, security, and a chance for a decent living," he says. The distant lands are rich green and are able to bring in millions of dollars in agriculture, drugs including opium and meth, and human trafficking. But the people do not have access to this wealth.

"¿Ya lo mataron?" This is how death is articulated in this part of the world. *They killed him already.* This is life here; the coarseness of it conveyed so matter-of-factly. It's not clear to me who they're talking about.

"That fellow wouldn't take any shit from anyone. A straight arrow," my cousin's brother says. "People like that don't last around here." They all agree.

Taxi drivers are good sources of information. They take the pulse of the community and have details about the state of the war, road closures, oncoming assaults, and other things relevant to survival. "They are moving in from all sides now," our driver says, referring to the cartel.

From this crosshatch of mountain valleys and rancho regions

surrounding Coalcomán, galleros come down from hidden places, usually around fiestas patronales, carrying stacks of money—the fruits of their harvests. They lay down bets on roosters and risk their fortunes in cockfights. The fighting rings are shaped by local politics and the place where men's fates are determined. They throw down money, deeds to their lands, and their lives. Roosters decide it all.

In "las oscuritas" of clandestine cockfights, lives are forfeited, disputes are resolved, and families are abandoned. Some people, like my grandfather, are left destitute. These are las jugadas that men feel they must play.

My cousins and the taxi man talk of the fallen families, those that pulled through generations of conflict and who are still fighting to change the way things are done around here. The drive is long on this rugged path through the teeth of Tierra Caliente's mountains. Out the window, I watch the grazing sheep until I fall asleep.

━━━

I wake in Aquila to the shrieks of tortilla-making machines. Aquila is a village that borders on insanity. It is a wild west guarded by armed cowboys and a precious gateway to the mineral-rich zones that are currently erupting in conflict. Here, any movement without my cousin is impossible.

A throng of crowing roosters are amplified by the mountains, their cries reverberating into the village. Fierce birds that await their day inside fighting rings and who take their owners with them. The horizon is glazed a dusty orange as we drive up to Rambo House—my cousin's family ranch.

"We love Rambo," my cousin says, pointing to a poster above his mother's shrine. Machine guns protect his mother's spirit and the people of this town. Heroic figures like Rambo mold the local consciousness. As we approach the house, a ferocious guard dog lunges toward me before being restrained.

"Just let her smell you so she knows you're okay," someone says.

Everyone is eating together at the back of the property. I join them and am introduced to kin from another kingdom. We share a meal of chorizo and coconuts before I am taken to a cold, dark room behind a grand medieval wooden door. Clearly, the room has not been occupied in years. I study the catre bed and turn it on its side to check for scorpions, snakes, and spells. I drop onto the handwoven cot and inspect this medieval prison cellar. I open a shutter and let in the light that makes the dust and mosquitoes in the air sparkle. I kick my shoes to alert any scorpions and see a campesino's straw hat and leather chanclas next to a hanging rosary.

Eventually I lie down, exhausted, cocooning myself in the handmade Mexican blankets that cover the bed. I trace their sacred weave work with my fingertips and consider my own weave work, piecing together fragments of a past that may be too frayed to work into anything whole.

An active hive of red wasps hangs above my head like a chandelier. It reminds me of my true place in this land: to keep watch over my thoughts, move slowly, and accept the things I can't change and must close my eyes to.

I struggle to sleep, ravaged by mosquitoes that burn my hands and feet with bites and wrestle me out of my dreams. The air is always alive, but especially at night when spiritual elements are thick as humidity. Latin American villages are saturated in roving spirits. I wake with some of them having passed into my sweat. In the middle of the night, I gather some clothes and take a shower in frigid water on the far end of the property.

Under the moonlight, I look in the direction of where I

think my grandfather might be, now only a small distance from here. I absorb what I can of him through the coastal, desert, and tropical winds, which later collide to provoke the most bizarre of dreams.

◆◆◆◆◆

I wake to the cries of children.

"Ma–*má*! Ma–*má*! Pa–*pá*! Pa–*pá*!"

I raise my head and open my eyes into the rising sunlight. "Ma–*má*!" Children in agony, I think. "Pa–*pá*." But when I look out the window, I see no children, just a colorful macaw. Human words escape from its beak, rolling off its tongue with ease. Roosters in the distance are already coo–coo–roo–cooing and powwowing in their splendor, and the macaw crows along with them. I tear my body from the thin placenta of my blanket, feeling like a different person after my night among the spirits. Outside my window is a luscious garden of tamarindo, cirian, guayaba, nansis, alondra, limón, guanabana, guamuchil, palma de coco, zapote, anona, vastago, jamaica, papaya, pina, and aguacate.

I think of Yakima and all its orchards. I think of how often I dream of buying up orchards simply for the pleasure of seeing them die, the pleasure of seeing the land restore itself to its true form without the assault of any man. I dream of acquiring all the plots that have ever caused harshness to the people who work on it and letting them die a slow death to avenge all the lives their owners destroyed for profit. I savor the day when the land will return to its natural state and people can begin to thrive in peace, free from intense labor. The apples will wither away to make room for all the desert wildflowers, eliminating the ways that men obstruct other men from achieving happiness.

I step out of bed and onto the dirt floor of Rambo House.

Shake any scorpions from my shoes. Outside, pit bull pups tear at their mother's teats, suckling her as she drags them across the yard.

My cousin sticks his head through the open window and tells me we have to go see some people about some things. Important people. He leads me through the silent streets, zigzagging deeper into the village, both of us trying to decipher the moods of the people who surveil us. Boys leaned over trucks go quiet as they let us pass. A smile and a wave give us clearance into unknown lands. We are going to meet El Huarachero, Pollero, and Carnicero. Moving softly down the mountain slope like rivulets of rain, we eventually reach and greet a group of men repairing dirt bikes and drinking beer in front of their houses. They are alchemists of motors, people who refashion lives out of old parts. One man's forearms are blackened with motor oil—the warrior paint of the working class. We shake hands. Another man's slit eyes meet mine and I sense him questioning the intention of my visit. We're invited to sit on wicker chairs and wait for the boss.

"¿Gallo, cómo estás?" They exchange hugs.

They make small talk, check in on one another. More importantly, they do not insult one another by refusing a drink, or by bringing up business before discussing family matters. An old man named El Panadero scrubs the grime from baking sheets and asks my cousin for advice on some matters.

"Then let's go get them," the boss interjects, finally emerging from the house. "He's robbed me of $50,000, and several others too in the village." He downs his beer. "Tell you what, help me come after him and you'll get your cut."

My cousin's head shifts in my direction, suggesting the matter be postponed. A biker slams his brakes in front of the house, picks up a backpack they've left out for him, slings it over his shoulder and races off.

"Think about it," the boss insists. Then he turns to me, discomfited by my silence. "Sabes, a mi lo que no me gustan son los pochos." He is telling me that he despises U.S.-born Mexicans like myself. Perhaps he can smell something bad in me, can sense that I have the look of one who lives without an origin. That I am someone who is lost in distant lands. He wouldn't be wrong.

I agree with him. I tell him that some of us have lost our way and that some of us never find it, falling for dreams that displaced us with their falsehoods. I tell him that there are others like me, searching for more accessible homes. This he likes hearing, and they all return to their festive postures, drinking and talking of gambling debts, upcoming cockfights, and remedies for things like dengue and indigestion. They bring out the foods that are specialties of this area.

"Javelina." Skunk pig and snake. "Cures for many ailments."

El Panadero serves it like a baguette. I unravel it from its paper wrap and inspect the jerkied rattlesnake in my hands. I put my nose to it and recoil on the inside. The men's eyes weigh on me.

Adam and Eve ate the apple. But I eat the snake.

⸺

Since my car accident I think more often about death, about the legacy I want to leave behind. I know that movement is critical to my survival and keeps me plugged into my surroundings and my history. Traveling forces me to rethink my relationship to the land and the baggage I have accumulated in my life. I extend this sense of movement onto my accordion keys. I use it to resuscitate words that have been stolen during my years living in the United States.

The more I flow alongside other men and experience their emotions, the more I think about how maybe this journey was never really about the accordion. Instead, it was about finding a camaraderie. As men, we need a pretext for breaking the barriers of loneliness, for seeking guidance in the ways of the heart. This is what the accordion has given me: a way to find my proper place inside myself and among good men.

By shadowing my cousin, I begin to learn that the way we move through this world can produce its own kind of music. He teaches me about the importance of going through motions together and not always doing everything alone. He dropped everything to stand beside me, to act as my guardian. He has endured the long days and nights with me, risked persecution from associating with outsiders in my presence.

Even when my journey is deeply personal, I do not always have to be alone.

DANZA DE LA CONQUISTA

TODAY, WE GO TO THE LOST TOWN OF COÍRI—LOST NOT ONLY TO PEO-
ple like me, but to almost everyone I know in Mexico—the place
where my grandfather was raised. Located on a steep mountain-
top, Coíri gives the illusion of being a village adrift on clouds.
It is an indigenous town that has fully preserved its sacred traditions. It's a place I must visit, to trace my story as far back as
I can go.

Coíri is where I must travel to absorb an energy that existed
long before my grandfather emerged from its forests. I must see
what my ancestors might have seen, before they experienced the
trauma of travel into foreign lands. I go there to reflect as they
might have reflected, to dream as they might have dreamed. I

go to immerse myself fully in what they might have lived and breathed ages ago, long before I entered this world.

In visiting, I hope to gain the confidence I need to confront my grandfather. I owe the gesture not only to my family, but also to myself. I owe it to my son, whom I will teach that there are sacred points on this land that must be experienced in our own unique ways, because they offer us an opportunity to confront the heavy things in our lives. Coíri is the birth source of my ancestors, but also a place of rebirth for myself. I cannot turn away from it.

A relative of mine, who works as a teacher, drives my cousin, his brother, and me through the country highways at full speed. On the drive, my cousins educate me on the indigenous territories of this region: Aquila, Pómaro, Coíri, Oztula, and Huitzontla. The scrappy car dodges gaping holes in the road, stopping the rhythms of my heart. The driver's eyes are glazed over, withdrawn, hard. He's obviously inebriated. Banda music blasts from our vehicle. Once again, I'm haunted by the feeling that this land will not permit me to escape with its story in hand.

My cousin's brother, who is also a teacher, tells me that Nahuatl and Purépecha are still spoken here, but very little—the government forbade people from speaking their indigenous languages for generations and forced them to speak Spanish instead. In these regions, like Pómaro, there are often many languages present. A number of these tongues still flow through the Álvarez strain, like Purépecha, but Nahuatl is the strongest. The presence of other languages in our family is as faded as they have become in these communities.

"We're trying to revive the language," he says. As a teacher in the indigenous lands of Pátzcuaro, he's teaching children their language as well as traditions like danza. "We still speak our languages here, primo," he tells me proudly.

We drive through the village of Estopila where big, ancient

trees are cut down by the maderos, generations of lumbermen. The wood is then burned, its smell permeating all of Michoacán, and is exported across the world for furniture. It is wood that never stains or ages and, when it burns, gives fire its deep red. Along another never-ending road is the town of Pómaro, a small indigenous community where the bloodline is still pure, says my cousin. "Sangre pura."

The drive drags on and the day grows darker. Just when I thought we were already in rugged lands, we enter the true backcountry. We struggle up dangerous cliffsides on neglected roads that have been beaten down by weather and mudslides. I'm beginning to lose faith in my cousin, beginning to doubt that there really is a town of Coíri at the end of this drive. We have already spent two and a half hours going up inclines so steep, they often send the car sliding back toward the cliff's edge.

"We keep these roads this way for a reason," my cousin's brother tells me. Coíri has long been a sanctuary for the persecuted and oppressed, an indigenous safe haven made safer by how hard it is to reach.

"Don't worry, we're almost there," they keep telling me.

These are roads like the ones where many family members of mine have been murdered, taken for a joyride by friends only to be betrayed, and I hate that I am letting myself fall prey to this old story. I begin rehearsing worst-case scenarios and making escape plans. I'm in the back seat, closest to a door that actually functions. An advantage. In one small jump, I could somersault into the dark jungle, taking my chances with the tarantulas, snakes, and ocelots. I slip my hand into my go-bag for the nuts and jerky that would sustain me.

"Don't worry," they keep telling me. But I worry. I can't help it. I was bred in worry.

Many hours later it appears: the village of Coíri. It's as if the earth cracks open just for us. A small village rises inside the soft haze of something like fog, everything bathed in an amber glow. I hear the distant tune of a danza beat. I stick my head out the window and inhale deeply. We are amid a forest of copal trees ,and their sacred sap thickens the air.

The music intensifies. It's coming from an old building in the town square, the only structure that's currently lit. When the car stops, I pursue this sound as if I'm under a spell. It leads me along a dark road.

Later, down the same street, I will enter the home of my cousin's grandpa, a keeper of the Nahuatl language who will reveal to me that he knows my own grandfather, Eulogio. Around here, my grandfather is known as "Jovenazo": the one who lives by the code of youthful adventure.

My cousin's brother accompanies me into the hall where indigenous youth are practicing la Danza de la Conquista, the ceremonial dance of the conquest. My grandfather used to live next door to this hall in the city square.

Their teacher is a man nicknamed "El Guero." He is about my height, with Spanish conquistador bone structure and an intense gaze. He is serious about taking back his lands from Spanish and Mexican destruction and instructs the youth in ways to revive old traditions, teaching them the history of the violence through danza.

The children dance in unison, smacking small sticks as if in battle. The music ricochets inside the large hall, ancient sounds circling back on themselves. It mixes like masa into the air, the children's feet kneading the sound. I consume it and taste the flavors of Coíri.

In the wake of the Mexican Revolution of 1910–1920, amid the disorder, a new kind of war erupted here in Tierra Caliente: a religious one. It was called the Cristero War and was financed by the Church against government persecution that ensued between 1926 and 1929. Articles had been introduced into the Mexican constitution to restrict religious activities, and the fight to separate church and state resulted in the slaughter and displacement of hundreds of thousands in Mexico. During that time, many of my relatives fled to the mountains, to villages like Coíri, or the United States as refugees.

"One day I will teach children la Danza del Machete," El Guero tells me—a dance with machetes. He wants to teach them never to shy away from their bloody past, but instead to confront it and chop tyranny's head off.

Outside the hall after class, we sit on the ground under a single light bulb as El Guero smokes weed. I'm moved by the majesty of this town. There's something familiar about this place, as if my spirit has been here before. Something feels right here, like it is the place where spirits migrate to meet in a council with the living elders. But it also feels like a forgotten place, forgotten even by many spirits. Something in the chain has been obstructed. The map to this place has been obliterated by violence.

"We must bring an end to these feuds, the bloodshed," El Guero says.

When we finish speaking, I thank him for sharing his knowledge and slink away.

My cousin's brother walks me through the quiet town square. "Primo, el aire de Coíri es el aire más puro del mundo." He insists that this air here is the purest in the world.

I clean my lungs with this celestial air and sit among the spirits that I can feel flowing among us here.

We approach a grand door to an old church.

"This, my father built," my cousin's brother says.

Here, doors are both works of art and spiritual endeavors. Craftsmen draw incredible patterns into fine wood. Doors delineate maps, a topography of one's household and one's commitment to the spiritual world. The door is the face, a first impression before someone enters a building. It sets the mood and gives a message to those wishing to enter, inviting them into the sacred space but also into the story the door itself tells. The call to heed the power of the door—its grain, its history—is also a way to reflect on the power that each of us carries, relinquishing our armor before entering, as equals, to share our spirits in community with those inside. Their thresholds are demarcations between what we think we are and what we can truly become. There was a time when my grandfather collected doors. He recovered them from construction jobs in the United States, giving them new life after they'd been abandoned.

We return to a small mud house to meet my elders, including my cousin's grandfather. One of my last living ancestors, he's now in his nineties. He is hard of hearing and reaches for my hand as if to understand me through the vibrations in my bones. After we communicate like this for a while, he smiles, finally recognizes my grandfather in me. Old souls finally reunited. He gives me a hug.

"I've been waiting for you," he says.

The elder speaks in Nahuatl to the children running around him, blanketing them in the magic of his words. His daughter brings me a glass bottle of what looks like damp soil. It's café mojo, a bitter local coffee bean. Here with café in the land of Coíri, I feel some peace inside of me. This will most likely be the last time I see this place. It takes a guide, a family, to see one safely through. It takes people like my cousin who put themselves at great risk moving outsiders into their lands, breaking the people's code to protect their ways.

We leave Coíri in the dead of night, driving blind and mostly downhill. My stomach drops at the thought of moving back down the treacherous hills at night and without seat belts.

The route is long and twisted. But we make it back to the coastal highway, which is long emptied and darkened by curfew. Our driver is weary, drunk, and swerving. He pulls off to the shoulder for more beers. He and my cousin drink down a few more to "combat sleep," they say, before the driver accelerates back onto the road at full speed, desperate to beat the encounters with gunmen or comunitarios who keep the order. Nighttime is when most confrontations happen.

But we aren't fast enough. We hit a roadblock and heavily armed men bring us to a stop. They are comunitarios and indigenous farmers equipped with AK-47s. My cousin tells me they are tired of seeing their people disappeared and butchered at night. We stop. The driver nervously rolls his window down and relief breaks over his face when the gunman recognizes him as a Nahuatl teacher in their community.

"¿Ya es muy tarde, no?" They're upset to see him out this late and on this road. They warn him about curfew, scold him, and finally let us pass.

Without people like him and my cousin, these lands would be inaccessible to me. Its history, my grandfather's story, my origins would be choked off from me as if by a tourniquet. I am thankful to have been able to see it.

But my chances of accessing any more of it are diminishing every day, along with the area's resources and the murdered and dying elders, who preserve the last of our story.

Finally, near midnight, we come back to Rambo House to rest. Like zombies, we disperse wordlessly to our separate quarters. I lie for a moment in a hammock in the half light of the moon, beneath the poster of Rambo. My feet sweep the dirt floor while I watch the pups piled into a corner, kicking the air as they experience nightmares of their own.

I retreat to my room and crawl into sleep, too tired to let the true experience of the day sink in.

UN EMPACHE

IN COASTAL, MOUNTAINOUS MICHOACÁN, MY COUSIN AND I RIDE THE deadly snakes of country roads toward my grandfather. We are caught behind the mining trucks that muscle their way through hostile territory, delaying us as they prepare to burrow down entire mountains. We press on toward the area of El Ranchito, near where my grandfather lives and close to where he abandoned my father, forcing him to live on the streets and beg for food. It is the place where my grandfather has lived for decades, keeping himself distant and free from the outside world. Here, things are coated in dust that gets kicked up by horses and conflict. It is a place layered in the past deeds of elders, a place where lawless men hitch themselves to taverns. It is where legacies begin and rope people like me back in.

I prepare myself to meet a man whose life may have extinguished him so much that he's no longer able to narrate it to me accurately. Whose life might not offer me anything I can use to repair myself. I must come to terms with the possibility of tragedy, with the chance that there is nothing extraordinary about my grandfather's story. At least not in the way I might expect.

I hold onto my accordion as a way to make sense of whatever mess I encounter. I prepare myself to finally discover whether I have pursued a real person or merely an illusion: a man who never existed in my life in any significant way other than his absence from it. At the moment when I'm about to meet him, I'm terrified to realize that there might be nothing to this journey. But I find strength in knowing that the accordion has already taken on so much life for me through my experience with others, with the makers and players and teachers who have aided me. My accordion has become so much more than a symbol of my grandfather. It holds all the musicians who've shared their stories, the relatives risking their lives to show me their lands, the landscapes I have absorbed while seeking answers to our family's history. I know that I have established a powerful relationship with my past, regardless of what I discover. I am prepared to let my accordion be only this. This is enough. My grandfather cannot take it away from me.

"You won't be staying the night at your grandpa's," my cousin says, though that's what I had originally planned. He doesn't elaborate. "It's not the right time."

I don't press him. We breach new lands, where banana plantations blanket the entire horizon. Clusters of bananas are encased in black plastic bags like the severed heads that sometimes turn up on these lands. Roadblocks control the flow of traffic into the town of El Ranchito. Military presence is everywhere and masked men prowl with machine guns drawn in anticipation of a new cartel assault.

When we finally reach my grandfather's place, we knock on

the rusted metal double door. I call out to him. No answer. After long moments of silence, when all I can hear is the distant cooing of roosters, I push the door open and we slip into the cave of a recluse.

"Abuelo," I call out. Still nothing.

The floors are bare except for a few clusters of ancient boxes. In the corner is a hammock with no one in it. Clothes are neatly strung up on a clothesline near a rusted bicycle. There's an old TV, an ancient fridge, a few pots and pans, some ancient chairs, tin cans, dismantled radios and electronics. A disarray of unfinished projects. It looks like the work of a madman, his experiments stretched across the floor and into corners, stacked up to the ceiling. Here is the work of a wandering mind, still curious and engaged in discoveries.

I step into a ray of light that filters in from the back of the house and look to where a wall and door should be. Outside in the backyard, I see a man caught in the web of a hammock like a giant spider. It's my grandfather, stretched out between trees and shaded by a forest of mango, ciruela, coyúl, guamúchile, aguacate, and yaca trees he has planted over the years. He's in a tank top and pants. He hears me coming toward him and he shifts his body upward, squats into his hammock, peers at us. Strangers to him still.

"Abuelo." I try to let my voice soften him as I walk toward him. He watches me, wide-eyed, then squints to study me more closely. His face is as wrinkled as a twisted towel. I watch as he finally wrings understanding from it. I am his boy's son come to dig out his past. His face lights up in a big smile. He opens his arms and I hug his frail bones.

"Your father said you'd come," he says before lying back down on his hammock and lighting another cigarette. "We have a lot to talk about," he says, "a lot to talk about." His breaths are slow and heavy. Talking seems to deplete him.

He invites us to sit down. "Aquí estoy, colectando años," he says. He has been here collecting the years, he says, as if harvesting them into his hand.

The man before me was born September 14, 1931, deep in the saltpeter mountains of the area. The mineral extracted from those mountains is used to make gunpowder and as part of an old practice for drawing out demons during exorcisms. This is the mineral in our bones. The fire that sleeps inside us. From these hot lands of Tierra Caliente, and its endless violent eruptions and civil war, came my grandfather, my father, and my origin story. I come from blood that gives me no rest.

He gestures slowly as he talks, his hands swimming through plumes of smoke. On a folding chair beside his hammock is a machete, a pack of cigarettes, a fly swatter, a slingshot, a blue long-sleeved shirt, and his walking stick.

My cousin seems more on edge than usual. Now and then, he raises his head to look around to where the car is, keeping an eye on the front door. He does periodic checks at the front of the house while my grandfather and I talk.

When he speaks, my grandfather has a soft voice. After a few minutes, he puts on his dress shoes and walks me toward a plant he calls "chan." It's a plant, he explains, that aids him with a pain in his stomach that he's been carrying for over fifty-five years. An "empache," he calls it—a word difficult to translate but that signifies some disturbance in the stomach that takes away his cravings. This loss of appetite can be caused by something bad you ate. He's had this ache all his life and he blames it on witchery.

The winds pick up and rattle the trees like maracas, making it difficult to hear his speech. It's as if the earth is erasing his words the moment he utters them, as if the winds know what my family believes: that there's no power behind what he says anymore.

I move in closer, conscious of the fact that in these lands I cannot speak the things I wish to speak. I cannot out myself to neighbors as his grandson. I cannot reveal that I am a grandson of anyone in this country. Once you leave these lands, you are forever an outsider, no longer a part of this violent tribe. We are in dangerous proximity to the homes of mob bosses, and I cannot shout the things that upset my own stomach and soul. Like asking him, the way I want to ask him, what he has to say about the long life he led and the people he turned his back on. What was it about his music that comforted him in ways his people didn't?

"Este empache," he says, "fue provocado por tu abuela."

Even now, he casts blame for his bad luck on others. Even now he sours the name of spirits he abandoned, like my father's mother, who died trying to give my father a better life. My grandfather believes his pain is a curse that she placed upon him many years ago. Perhaps it's the closest he can get to an admission of guilt.

My cousin suddenly can't stop sneezing.

"Ven aca," my grandfather says, instructing him to open his palms. He spritzes them with some spray of alcoholic herbal mixtures and tells my cousin to inhale deeply. "That should cure you."

My grandfather sits back in his hammock and I watch him, living the last of his dreams, slowly fading away until the day he will slip into another life, leaving me and the rest of my lineage to collect the stories.

He appears to remember something and gets up using his walking stick. He grabs a bag of trash that he then sets over a chan bundle, sprays with alcohol, and sets alight into a ball of fire.

"Yo era muy bailarín," he says, his eyes on the fire. Back in the day, he loved to dance the pain away, to beat back the empache, he says. "Me gustaba mucho bailar y montar lobos."

Loved to dance and ride wolves, he says. Living dangerously and recklessly. He says strange things sometimes. I was warned about this. He has things to say and I let him say them one last time, to the few members of his family who still stand by and listen.

"Abuelo, I wanted to ask you about your music. About your accordion."

He looks away, takes a long moment, tells me that was ages ago. "Se me pudrió de gusanos," he says, telling me his music had decomposed, and his accordion was tunneled by maggots. He quickly drops the subject, moving on to stories he is more interested in telling.

I feel cheated somehow, robbed of the opportunity to engage in something deeper with my grandfather. We exchange no meaningful conversation about the accordion or the people he has hurt. He only offers braggadocio about his disastrous life and expects me to just listen.

Suddenly I feel this instrument as a hindrance, this journey a waste of time. *Maybe I will never play this thing again,* I tell myself. But then I remember all the effort that I have already put into learning it, all the lives that have been shared with me because of it. I think of Broussard and Poullard and the others and what the instrument has meant to them. Though my grandfather was never my teacher, I am freed from any rigorous instruction he might have imposed on me as the only way to learn. I am not beholden to any tradition or genre and can partake of many of them, eventually passing down the accordion and its accumulated stories to my son and others who are learning to play.

I have learned that the accordion makes family out of strangers and ghosts out of injurious family members. It has placed me on the path to finding the right people in my life.

"I have something to show you," he says, and he walks into his house, stepping tenderly as if on glass. He comes back and drops something into my lap before stretching back out into his hammock to smoke.

He has handed me two credentials of some sort. The first is a form of identification proving his affiliation with La Union Nacional de Detectivos Mexico. A detective in Mexico City, dated January 11, 1971. When my own father was roughly nine years old in Michoacán, starving, and my grandfather was forty years old.

There was another time, my grandfather tells me, when he worked as a young journalist for a police magazine called *Argos*. The history and purpose of the magazine are obscure to me, but it seems to be a sort of noir publication containing illustrations and essays on police and crime.

I wonder at the material that was possibly written by my grandfather, the images that emerged from his pen. Perhaps there are stories I could study, looking for clues in their characters that might eventually reveal to me a more human narrator. Something more nuanced than this old-fashioned cowboy who still seems to be stuck in the past.

My grandfather sighs. "Look at me now. Surrounded by una bola de pendejos." He grieves about the cartel that lives on every side of him. "If they found out what I used to be . . ." He looks around cautiously.

I review his second credential, which is as chewed up and sepia-stained as the first one. Sure enough, it states that at age thirty, my grandfather was a reporter for the "Revista Policiaca Argos." In large letters, adjacent to his reporter's credentials, it reads:

"La mejor de las armas es LA PALABRA ESCRITA
Debéis usarla con honor y dignidad
En defensa y engrandecimiento de
La cultura y de la Patria"

It says that the best weapon is the written word and should be used with honor and dignity in defense and aggrandizement of the culture and the homeland. Words are our weapons. So is the lack of them. But journalism was a way of life that did not sustain him. Though he was a writer first, he later turned in his pen for a gun when he joined the ranks of detectives during one of many tumultuous periods in Mexico's history.

I can feel my window of opportunity closing; my portal to the past is shrinking quickly. I say what I can, but my tongue still cowers from asking him what our true source of strength is. From asking him how I can be stronger in this life. But what words could satisfy generations of unanswered questions? What reasons could this man possibly have that would justify his actions in the past? No, this man cannot be rushed. He was never rushed back then, and he will not be rushed now.

Much of our exchange takes place in silence, in our glances. I lean toward him and try to feel his faded aura. This is the fundamental contradiction of our lives: even though I have found him after all these years, he is still not really here. He is still somewhere far away, disengaged and self-absorbed in the treasures of his past.

Once again, I feel as though my journey has been for nothing. My image of him might have remained stronger had I kept my distance. Always, the closer I get to him, the further he recedes. Here I am at the source of our family cosmos and yet feeling further than ever from the answers I was looking for. By pursuing him, I have done the polar opposite of what my father wanted. Now, my grandfather and I are sharing in a moment that was never meant to happen. A moment that I forced to happen, against all signs that hinted I should quit this pursuit.

My presence seems to register with my grandfather as nothing out of the ordinary. There isn't much visible change in him that I can read to indicate either enthusiasm or unease. Perhaps at his age few things are capable of piquing his interest. When he does muster what little energy he can, it's to relay bits of his adventures and to conveniently edit his past. I cannot help but feel like a dirty vessel, just a body for stories to be dumped into as a way to cleanse his name. As though my purpose is to absorb the way he sees himself and carry the few pieces he hands me back to my world and my family. I hate that I have to sit here and listen to his stories that admit no responsibility for his past.

At the same time, I know it may very well be our last opportunity to be together. So I wait out this closing portal, allowing myself to experience this moment slowly and softly, on my grandfather's terms. He draws out what sense he can from his long life and I watch it unfold in front of me, feeling pain for him and no sense of resolution for myself.

As he speaks in obscure words, he keeps coming back to the idea of his secret treasure. He wants to map out its location. To him, this is his contribution, his gift, his legacy—some treasure that will never be found. This is what he leaves behind: a map, a fantasy. We all have a similar dream, the idea of a goal we must pursue that gives our life meaning. We must live with the sense of always seeking it but knowing we may never fully recover the answers. In this way, I am thankful to my grandfather, who has at least maintained a vigorous imagination. In this way, we are one, both equally and enthusiastically lost.

No one in my family has ever had the answers to our past, not even my grandfather. I am foolish to have believed otherwise. Instead, I must absorb as many precious moments with him as I can.

My family lives against the friction of our existence, doing our best to excavate ourselves from pain—even if we have caused this pain ourselves. Somehow, I must find strength in this tumultuous legacy.

The silence between me and my grandfather is abruptly shattered. My cousin has received a call.

"Noé, we have to go," he tells me after hanging up. "Get your things." We have to leave my grandfather's place immediately. "We'll be back tomorrow."

Unbothered, my grandfather drops back gently into the embrace of his hammock, throws his arm back, and blows smoke into the beating sun. To him, this departure has already been written.

FALSE GOLD

FIRST THING THE NEXT MORNING, WE'RE BACK ON THE TIGHT AND dangerous highways, bobbing and weaving around military trucks. We're on our way toward El Ranchito to see my grandfather again, driving in another shitty borrowed car. We swerve against oncoming traffic, navigating high precipices, shaving off more of our luck. The gearshift keeps getting stuck and sending our wheels spinning. Tarantulas dash across the road. As we press into the shaggy jungles, I notice that the mood of the town has changed. There is no military installed today. No protection. It is the calm before the storm. We pass a sign tagged with the words MICHOACÁN ESTÁ EN TIEMPO DE LA LUCHA. *Michoacán is in a time of struggle.*

Again, we knock on my grandfather's door and again there is

no answer apart from a faint radio. Again, I slip my hand inside the metal door where a knife has been wedged and once more we find my grandfather in the back, cocooning in his hammock.

"That will be my new garden," he says, turning off his radio and pointing to garden plots bordered by leaves.

This time, I carry the accordion case in my hand. I see him notice it, see him watch as I set it down beside him. He says nothing about it. Instead, he leans back into his hammock, takes a long inhale of smoke and gives a contemplative look to the bright sky as he begins to talk. Always talk; never listen. As before, I let him say the things he wishes to say. He releases the bitter words that still burn holes through his stomach and I listen, hoping it might finally bring him peace to know there's someone strong enough to meet him with kindness.

"People here are like rabbits," he says, crouching closer toward me on his hammock. "They're small, dumb, and con orejas muy grandes," with very big ears. He tells me people are always surveilling him and that he's smart for avoiding their detection all these years. "I keep to myself. I prefer it that way."

He sees me looking at a dusty bicycle in the back and he tells me he can no longer ride because he was run off the road by someone in the family. He crouches closer, instructs me to keep quiet about what he's about to say. I'm surprised by how heavily he lays it on: "Because this is the last time I'm seeing you, I have to tell you before it's too late. I'm on the trail of the man who was hired to murder your father's mother." My father's mother, as I have always heard it, had been tossed from a moving truck and left for dead many years ago. This investigation is something he says he still hides from my father. It's the first I'm hearing of this and it tears at my heart. I try to swallow but it lodges in my throat like a fish bone. This information, I know, I cannot pass on to my father. This is not the path any of us needs to be on.

Gradually, I begin to see it for myself—the paranoia in his

eyes and the destruction playing out in his mind. Slowly, painfully, I begin to understand why so much of my family's past was buried, meant to be forgotten.

"I want to give you something," he says. He asks my cousin to leave us alone for a minute. He pulls out a pen and paper and uses my accordion case as a table, uninterested in its contents. Crouching over it, he begins to draw. "I want you to have this map," he says—the map to his famous Spanish gold. He takes me through a labyrinth of details to the source, a site he said he visited before but can no longer do so safely, given the conflicts that abound in the region.

He sketches out all the rivers and mountains that must be crossed, mentions the structures and the trees that signal the specific location. I consider his lifelong search for this treasure that did nothing but impoverish him. That might impoverish me too.

As he draws his treasure map in all its confusing details, I see in him something painful. I see in him what I've observed in my many years of working in shelters for unhoused people. I see that this man has a troubled mind—perhaps was even born with it. I have also seen a similar pattern play out with a brother of mine. I realize that I may have found the missing piece in my family history—that there was a sickness that destroyed his ability to live well. Seeing it now, it breaks my heart. The paths that he traces out don't offer a route to his treasure, but a map of his own afflicted mind. In the end, no one could tell me his story because I don't think anyone knew it, not even him. Mental health was certainly not something that was talked about in Mexico in those times.

Everywhere I turn is filled with tragedy. So much life is violently interrupted, my grandfather's included. Suddenly, I feel incredibly thankful for all that my parents did to save me from this place. It is clear that escaping was what worked for my family, displacing themselves so they could find something new.

This realization offers me a different way to think about my own restless movement—to travel so that our old stories don't reach me. Now that I'm here, I see that I was never meant to return to this country, at least not to these harmful parts. There's a reason it was so difficult to get to this place. But I made it my mission to pry. I wanted to see these stories for myself before I decided whether I should abandon them.

Witnessing the extreme suffering in Mexico is a lot to bear alone. The truths that I'm privy to are still unavailable to my extended family. It's hard to be the one to ask questions about where we came from; hard to hear the answers and to hear that, sometimes, there are no answers. It is tough to inhabit this twisted family legacy, the legacy of a region that was kept from me throughout my childhood. I worry that I have violated some sacred order by digging up a part of my father's story I was never meant to see, despite his blessing.

I pocket the treasure map.

"Abuelo, I brought you something," I finally say. He watches me lean over the case. I open it and let my accordion finally take root in his land, to absorb whatever vibrations still live inside of him. I ask him to play something.

He puts it on gently with my assistance. As the instrument comes into contact with his body, I see something light up in his eyes, as if he's reliving old dreams. They brighten even more as he scans the button keys with his fingertips. I keep hold of his weak frame so the weight of the accordion does not crush him.

He dips his ear to it, tries to pull from it sounds and patterns that he has long outgrown. Still, he finds his chords and sings about "bailando bonito." About dancing freely over this earth again.

It's a beautiful thing to see a man reacquainted with an old emotion, with the spirit of a thousand songs. As he plays, I see more clearly the tragic beauty of his adventures, his courage to stay curious and explore. I take from him what I imagine he can provide, even though he cannot offer me the answers in reality, and commit it to the instrument.

At last, I feel a sense of accomplishment in my journey. I have gotten the accordion into his hands. It was important to me that he touch it, that he use it to produce his own sounds. It was also important for me to stir the spirits here and to let them know that things are different now. That we are not bound to this place in the way we once were. Here, finally, is where I ask the spirits to let us go now and to be at peace. And to be kind to a grandfather who brought so much destruction to others.

This is why I pursue the accordion: as a reminder of what it takes to build love and community for oneself and one's family. It is a template for rethinking my relationship to my people and to myself. The accordion and its complex processes of playing and craftsmanship keep me mindful of the hard work, the discipline, the passion that I must dedicate to my family. Especially in my new role as a father.

Some stories are hard to track down for a reason. There are people in our lives who for good reason do not want to be found, and there are certain ghosts that prefer not to be disrupted. In tracking down my grandfather, I have found that some ancestors can be a hindrance to us. I thought I would never find peace without knowing his story. But holding on too tightly to old pictures, old memories, and pursuing frayed relationships can actually hold us back from achieving spiritual liberation. There's something scary in relinquishing our ancestors, in severing ourselves from certain parts of our history. But there's also something powerful and exciting about starting anew, about testing the limits of the person you think you can become, without the tragedy of the past to obstruct you.

In the end, I didn't gain that much from my short encounter with my grandfather. But I am thankful for the person I grew into during my crazy pursuit of this *idea* of a grandfather, and the bonds I formed with other musicians on the path to him. I am thankful for the family darkness that has driven me to confront my tender spots, for the demons that I could never quell but that provoked me to assert myself in this world. The pursuit fortified me. I am not lost just because I never fully grasped my grandfather's story.

Now, I watch my grandfather struggle to give air to an instrument that is clearly overpowering him. "An accordion must always be played standing up," he says, but standing up is hard for him under the box's weight. I hold him for balance as the music diminishes his energy. I see him digging deep inside himself for the music that has long since left him, cocking his ear to the distant voices only he can hear. It is hard to watch someone in their most vulnerable state, like watching a dying animal. It is hard to witness my own story coming to an end here, in this way. Here, a part of me dies.

MAMALONA

(Houston)

"YOUR GRANDFATHER IS NOT WHO YOU THINK HE IS."

After Mexico, I visit with an aunt in Houston who helps me set the story straight. If Mexico is where my family's story began, Houston is where it ends, where my family's truth lives. The city is home to an aunt of mine I've never met before, but who I want to speak to because she endured many years with my grandfather. It was my father who suggested I meet with her. Before visiting with her, I wanted to see Mexico and my grandfather for myself. I wanted to reckon with my own emotions first, before I saw the full picture of someone else's experience. Houston would be the place that would give context to what I saw in Mexico.

My tía Estela is my father's long-lost sister. They were only reunited in adulthood, when my father traveled to California in response to a letter Estela wrote to him. Estela pulls up at the Greyhound station in her big black mamalona—what they call trucks in Houston, she tells me.

"Jump in." Her rolled-up sleeves expose hard muscle and tattooed forearms. Her face holds the story and the struggles of a mother of three; someone who fought with all her might to support her children and give them a different life than the one she had. The car smooths over a grand landscape of concrete, miles and miles of it.

I am welcomed into a house in mourning. Her son was recently gunned down under a bridge.

"I left his car and room the way it is," she tells me. "That way he will always be with me." She touches a picture of her son's face on our way to the room where I'll be staying.

An area of the house is dedicated to her crafting, where she makes prints for T-shirts to give to her friends. The work keeps her busy and saves her from falling apart in her grief. There are spools of yarn and fabric and sewing machines for making outfits and costumes. Eclectic in her tastes, she believes in the power of fabrics to influence good emotions, she says. Being conscious of the way she dresses helps her shape-shift into the identity she was long denied when living under my grandfather's rule in Mexico.

She likes pushing back on society's ideas of a woman's place in the world, she says. "I'm my own woman and I try to do what makes me happy." As we bond over food, I am moved by the beautiful spirit before me.

"I came out here long ago, to be away from it all. Away from all the family that wasn't there for me in my hardest times. From people who pull you down in life. To be where nobody knows me, here in Houston." Her words are delivered with confidence. They carry the bite of a fighting spirit.

Already we're a lot alike, I feel, in our shared desire to remove ourselves from the strain of trauma.

"If only we had met earlier, mijo."

I agree with her. Knowing her sooner would have offered me a model: a different and perhaps better way to live. For hours we bond over all the lost time between us, building what we can of our relationship after my father spent years searching for her. She puts her hands on the fabrics of some shirts piled on a table. "I like to help people, to make them happy with my gifts." I watch her engage with the things that bring her peace, admiring the courage it takes to continue fighting after her recent loss.

She is eager to put the pieces of the story together for me, to help solve this mystery of who my grandfather really was. As she speaks, I am pulled in by the spell of the two worlds that raised her: Mexico and the United States.

"Your grandfather moved me between Mexico and California," she says. She and her mother lived under the hard rules of a man who was always angry and perpetually in hiding, withdrawn inside his tumultuous mind and torrential spirit. The damaging effects fell squarely upon my aunt. "I lived the life of a servant girl to other families in Mexico, family members who didn't want me around because I was the mistress's daughter." She describes the racism she experienced because of her indigenous blood and features, the racism against indigenous people in Mexico in general, and the struggles she had even among whiter relatives. She was blamed for my grandfather's multiple infidelities, targeted for having broken up marriages and families. Though my grandfather created the destruction, she endured its wake. "Your grandfather was jumping from roof to roof . . . trying to get at women," she says. "Your grandfather had many families across the land and took responsibility for none. He didn't care about anyone."

My romantic notion of a restless journeyman who spent his nights floating on the marina, serenading the moon with his accordion, is overwritten by this darker image. I was wrong. The boat that I thought carried an honorable man instead carried something deeply shameful.

"Your grandfather and my mom moved to San Diego, where she got pregnant with me. It was my mother who found a job with some Germans who owned a boat. Not your grandfather." They let him live at their house so her mom could babysit their two girls. "Your grandpa was always gone, clubbing from here all the way down to Guadalajara. My mom had to support herself without him."

The true power belonged to her mother, a pregnant woman who eked out whatever living she could to create a life for my aunt. But the Germans had employed him constructing parts for boats, she says. "That part was true.

"Your grandfather had us living in San Diego because it was close to Mexico. It was during the Vietnam War and he didn't want any of his family drafted, so he took his children to be born in Mexico."

He wanted an easy out. But in Mexico, Estela's life had hardly been easy. Working as a household cleaner, she served and scrubbed and polished people's ugly surfaces. She cleaned up after their messes the same way she cleaned up after the many temperamental men in her life and soaked up her mother's tears. For years, she scrubbed on hands and knees and dreamed of becoming her own woman.

"I did my best to live a happy life," she says. She compares herself to the doll she dragged around in Mexico that she had brought from the United States when her father uprooted the family in her youth. "I'm like her, Pippi Longstocking. I like her story because she lived with a father who was always away." Like Pippi's, Estela's father was always lost at sea, albeit in a sea of his own delusions.

Her mother also endured many dark moments, including at

the shoe shop where my grandfather had worked. "He got my mother a job there," she says, "really, to keep watch over her. At two dollars an hour, she was responsible for 'las suelas y los tacones'—gluing soles to shoes. She'd work las máquinas and would come home with glue stuck on her hands." Tía Estela would tend to her mother's hands, removing the glue from them and wishing she could likewise unglue her mother from the bad world they were living in.

"There was also the theater," she says. The cinema's Cuban owners employed my grandfather as a projectionist and also provided a room in the theater for his family to sleep in. My aunt and her mother adored the movies.

The phone rings in the middle of our conversation. It's Estela's mother calling from California, where she still lives. Estela puts her mother on speakerphone and asks her to share her own memories of their time in the theater. Estela motions for me to keep silent. "Her boyfriend doesn't like her talking with other men," she whispers.

"It had a stage for live performances," her mother recalls. "I remember sometimes the actors would leave behind their costumes and I would take them and cut them up with a knife to make clothes for you. We had no money to buy you clothes." She refashioned the material into new looks for her daughter, who lived inside the glorious images of other, safer worlds that films provided. Outside the world of the movies, she and her mother would cry themselves to sleep during my grandfather's outbursts.

Estela mutes the phone and whispers to me, "My mother gave birth to me on the floor of our home in California." She hid her contractions, and much of the birth, from my grandfather, who had already made it clear that he wanted his kids born in Mexico. While her mother was pregnant, she'd gone to live in a casa de huéspedes—a boardinghouse for sex workers—because her husband had taken off again. When she returned to the California house, Estela says, "She delivered me [herself] and cut her own umbilical cord."

"When your father came," Estela's mother says to her, "he was stunned. He didn't know what to do. He just sat back and smoked." He swirled in the familiar fog that detached him from responsibility to this world and the well-being of others. The next day, an ambulance took her to the hospital to be evaluated.

"I was born firmly to this land," Estela says, "among the grime and dirt left behind by men." She would commit her life to unearthing beauty from these toxic landscapes.

My mind swirls amid the details of my grandfather's violent, tragic trajectories. He is a man I'm ashamed to be connected to by blood. I've spent so long trying to find meaning in his story, and what Estela tells me suggests there is none to be found. These are my true origins: bad blood, the ugly nature of men.

I look back on it all, at all that I carried about my grandfather, and I feel disgust.

"But, mijo," my aunt insists, "don't stray from what you're doing, from the beautiful journey that you're on. After all, we would never have met if it weren't for your desire to dig at our family's past."

She's right. It all started with that picture of my grandfather with an accordion and a smile—an image that burrowed into my mind, that gripped me with its mystery and launched me on a journey. I had, in the end, still done what I'd set out to do: to discover the truth of who my grandfather really was. I was beginning to understand that my father, who was torn from a happy life by a father who abandoned him, might have met even more destruction had my grandfather remained in his life.

In uncovering the layers of our story, I must also confront the people my grandfather hurt. This has been a kind of gift. I once thought I might find my warrior spirit in my grandfather—a man who was never there for me, who never came searching for me or my father, who never inquired about the well-being of our family. Instead, I have found it in an aunt in Houston.

I sit with my aunt in our shared desire to piece ourselves together again.

My journey has opened my eyes to a lot of pain. Often, when I've said my goodbyes to the people I've met, they thank me and tell me how I filled a gap in their lives, when I only expected them to fill a gap in mine. Many of the soul-deep conversations I've had seem to have unclogged various hurts. In talking with others who have looked back to their childhoods and reevaluated their own relationship to their past, I have realized that though the past informs me, it does not define me. Sometimes I'm overcome by the depth of the tragedy in people's lives. But these are also the spaces where I want to dwell. I want to immerse myself in the pain of others in order to truly see the world around me.

On our last day together, my aunt and I hop into her mamalona and go to a print screening shop in town. She's going to make me a shirt. Together, we browse the aisles.

"Pick your colors," she says.

As a parting gift she passes on her wisdom to me in the form of a shirt that says "Elevate People."

I carry this message forward, vowing to elevate people in everything I do.

I leave Houston in a haze. On my way back to the Greyhound station, I feel as though I can see myself reflected in the many passersby. Do they know that I wish to know them? It is because of them, because of the many lone walkers, that I know love. I have to believe that my pain can be dissolved by moving within the flow of a community. All I have to do is to look up from my feet to see the others there with me.

I board my bus and sit swaying inside, letting myself be carried away like the many musical migrants who carried their instruments across grand landscapes. As I carry my heavy bag from bus to bus, state to state, country to country, I wonder what compelled migrants to pack their accordions for treacherous journeys, to commit to the weight of such an instrument. I have come to consider the accordion as a companion for the lonesomeness of travel. Perhaps its ancestral connection to the land one abandons is why people carry it. It helps with the loneliness, the heartbreak of detaching yourself from family, and gives us the power to speak our pain when we are at our most isolated.

CUTTING DOWN DEMONS

AT HOME, BACK IN SEATTLE, I RETURN TO THE WAREHOUSE WHERE I work in furniture delivery. Early in the morning, in the southern district where I break up crates and tear up boxes, I reflect on my purpose. I sit in a cold warehouse, listening to the sounds of staple guns erupting over luxury furniture. They blend in with the sounds of accordion music blasting from radios. Corridos set the pace and rhythms for the tapiceros—the migrant upholstery workers. They work and rework the fabrics, slipping new skins over old furniture to revive them with colors. The accordion finds its step among the echoes of the warehouse, softening the life of routine the way it has always done.

I sit on a truck bed between deliveries. Our team has broken for lunch on some random road. While I eat, I reflect on how the accordion took root in Seattle under the vaudeville tradition that emerged from the taverns and saloons of New York and San Francisco seaports. Seattle is a city that prospered from timber and the Klondike Gold Rush and promoted itself as the gateway to the rich resources of Alaska, Yukon, and Asia. The Orpheum Circuit, a chain of vaudeville theaters, featured the talents of immigrant performers like Italian accordionist Guido Deiro, who played during the Alaska-Yukon-Pacific Exposition of 1909. Throngs of working-class immigrants came to the Northwest to see Guido—the man who first popularized piano accordions in the United States. In my own way, my playing is a way to resuscitate this past and mix it with the experiences of contemporary immigrants, contributing my own sounds and mythologies to the city's salty air.

Later, back at the warehouse, I stand among a chaotic pile of boxes. We work in between the many truckloads that snake up to the warehouse door to unload crates while corrido music wafts through the air. Cool autumn winds move over my sweaty face, carrying the sounds of a busy city. Here in the warehouse, we listen to the lyrics of legends, like Los Huracanes del Norte's "Vaciando Botellas" (emptying bottles). It's a song about a man drowning down his sorrows in a cantina. His life has failed him so deeply that he keeps drinking so as to not feel his impending death.

I attack the cardboard with a box cutter. I skin the plastic wrap from the cardboard, imagining that it contains all the things I've bottled up over the years. I bury my blade in its dermis, cutting long wounds along its edges to release the pressure inside of it, inside of me. I cut my traumas into large cardboard squares and I pile them into a corner to be discarded. I exert myself until it's hard to move. We tussle with the boxes the way we do our many demons, embodying our frustrations until it becomes an art form, a way of life. Because we have no other choice.

Every day my coworkers and I expend our pain into the world using our backs and our hands, in silence and in song. We wield our box cutters like the gaucho knife fighters who dealt with their problems in blood. We fight against the flood of boxes, cutting open a space for ourselves and for our dignity.

When I can, I sit my tired body down onto rolled-up rugs, staring down at my feet and tracing the cracks in the concrete. One day this country will no longer be able to sustain the weight of our dreams. I think about the journeys that started with the lie that my grandfather might have been someone special, and the truths that that lie eventually brought me to.

I think of my música norteña, the deep cries of it that echoed in the apple orchards where my parents labored. All my life, I have been submerged in these sounds. The quivers of the accordion have always been my guide through the waters of the world, a world that would not let me speak my pain in Spanish. The men of norteño and their singing voices grounded me in my cultural reality, reminding me that I belong to two worlds. They were men who took pride in themselves and who turned their poverty into power, singing proudly of their humanity despite all the obstacles they faced.

The music is so much more than what my grandfather was. It is a source of strength far more powerful than any one person.

LAST DANCE

WHEN MY LITTLE BOY IS AFRAID, WHEN HE IS AWARE THAT HE HAS
ventured a little too far, when he turns to look for a soft embrace,
I hold him tightly, chest to chest, and hum a couple of *ya-ya-ya-
ya-ya*s to pass down the gentle tremors of my heart into his. He
feels the rhythms. We communicate heart to heart, and it paci-
fies him. When his body is clasped to mine, the warmth builds
between us like two embers. *Ya-ya-ya-ya-ya.* I hold him in these
sounds, give him a little bit of myself, until he falls asleep on my
chest and we merge into one another's dreams.

In moments like these, I feel assured in my job as a father.
But it's challenging to step into the role of fatherhood, to become
the person I so judged my father for being. It's hard to live up
to the person I always wanted my father to be—a happier, less

resentful one. Someone who could smile more at his children. I still feel deeply shaped by the things that shaped him. It's hard to escape from his shadow, his demons.

When I look at my boy, I find myself in the middle space between his face and my father's. I pull away from the parts of my past that caused me pain and confusion, and I push my boy toward new horizons that will better feed his heart and soul.

I try to be conscious of not unloading my family's tragedies onto my boy. Instead, I push myself into different patterns. I transfigure myself with smiles, reshaping my face and eyes at my boy so that he doesn't pick up on my sadness. I try to convey the warmer inner space of my spirit. I try to revive the muscles that have atrophied over the years and teach my boy a better way.

It is up to me to hold back as many ghosts as possible, so that my son can carry a lesser burden than the one I had. Through my experience of fatherhood, I am driven to let them go.

I see the pace at which my boy fights to grow into the person he wants to become. I see him accelerating into his own selfhood—his determination to walk, how he eagerly jumbles the sounds in his mouth that will become his first words. In all these advances, I am pressed to keep up with him. I am inspired to move inside this world the way he does, slowing down to take in these experiences as if they were once again new to me.

I think about the impact of my personal journey on my boy. How my tendency to travel in pursuit of self-discovery might perpetuate the pattern of abandonment. Striking out on my own is different now that I am a father—there are ways it might impact my relationship with my son. I don't wish to continue the family fragmentation, but I also see this act of departure as part of a sacred ceremony. If it's my way of processing the world, then I must communicate that fact with my loved ones, the way my grandfather never did. The key is to always come back to your family.

I carry my boy in everything I do now. Fatherhood has forced me to slow down and face the things I have always run from. All my dreams and concerns are now embodied in this small boy who is here to remind me that there is another way to live. I dip my fingers gently over my son's rib cage to elicit a quick burst of laughter. I draw out his giggles deliberately, hoping to loosen the knot of any hidden temper that may already be brewing inside him. The same temper that brews inside me, that brewed in my father.

I am also committed to showing him Yakima, hoping it will offer him a different narrative than the one I grew up with. I venture back to visit family. I continue to return to Yakima even though my father has always warned me that coming back will be the end of me. That it will chip away at me until it brings me to my knees like it does everyone. For years he cautioned me to keep myself away from the curse that is this land, the curse of inescapable human toil. He tells me that my place must be elsewhere. There are elements here that are destined to hurt me, he still warns to this day, and only in keeping myself away have I delayed the inevitable pain. His truth is spot-on.

All my life he has helped guard me from the harm that keeps hold on our family. When he stresses that my life will be better in the faraway, it makes me think of my grandfather. I think about how, in some cases, it is better for a man to remove himself in order to make room for things to grow.

For decades I have listened to my father and kept myself physically, emotionally, and spiritually distant. In so doing, I have denied myself many opportunities. Though I have visited Yakima many times, I have kept myself from building anything meaningful there. In keeping with my father's wisdom, I have tried to thrive in a way that my parents can be proud of and to keep from contributing any more harm to their lives. But living this way has also been a burden to me. And perhaps it is because of my yearslong absence that I am stuck inside of an old story, stuck to an old Yakima whose memories still wound me. For too long, I have denied myself the chance to reexperience my homeland in the way I deserve.

Months after my trip to Mexico, my journey with the accordion and distant elders complete, I return to my hometown to visit my parents and to fish the river with my father.

Under a dying sun one Saturday evening, I decide to take the car out into the Yakima desert. My baby boy has been put down to sleep at my mother's place. As I leave the house, I can feel late spring stretching into summer. I blast the music as I drive.

At a red light, a car next to me snarls its engine. For a stretch of road, we race with our hearts in our throats before coming to a stop at a red light, where I turn to face a group of high school boys. They are crammed into the car and cheering, enthralled as I am by the power of this moment in a land that offers almost nothing else. We grasp at the feeling of flight, as if racing fast enough might transport us elsewhere. I give them a smile and a thumbs-up, thinking of the years when I too put down my miles on these roads that lead to nowhere. I want to linger, to tell them that things will be hard but okay.

The lights turn green and I flash two fingers in a peace sign before they race off. I let them take the lead in a world that is no longer mine. This town that I relinquished long ago fills me with remorse. These boys, who embody the future, race past me and into that future. They will sort out this life in Yakima all on their own, without people like me who failed to figure it out. Down the road, I cruise past the boys again, when they are just about to turn a corner. They send me back an unexpected hand gesture in return: one of love, of peace.

I drive on, navigating by feel through the surrounding landscape, surrendering to the push and pull of sleepy streets. I empathize with everything I see: boarded-up homes, thirsty trees, all the countless human exertions we must make in order to survive. I slip back into the past, into the streets that grow more saturated with stories of hard-laboring families every year. I offer moments of silence to these structures steeped in love and tragedy. I cross the familiar wounds of train tracks, watching clusters of unattended kids walking on hot pavement. They are embarking on adventures just like I did on similar nights. My heart goes out to them, to the discoloration in their clothes. To the version of myself I see in them.

The houses here seem like embodiments of their occupants— struggling to keep themselves afloat. I try not to feel guilty that I didn't stay in Yakima, or that I couldn't do more while I was here to help its people. As I cruise through its landscape, I see for the first time that these drives have always been a way to mourn the things I couldn't fix, even when I was younger and still lived here. They were things that many young people feel powerless over. Now, as I drive, I mourn a boyhood I have long since abandoned. I see myself again with the homies, turning once again to the streets to try to find adventures and connection.

For the first time, I get a glimpse of something like closure. Only now do I understand how much drifting through the Yakima streets meant to me and my friends; how it informed my life. I see how profoundly alone I used to feel, and how this kind of cruising gave me the liberty to feel and be myself. I see too how profoundly in love I still am with the spirit and heartbreak of this town.

I feel myself tear up. I let the playlist resound even more loudly through me, shake me from my hardness. For the first time, I experience genuine love for a home that is no longer home and a land that is no longer my land.

I think back to earlier in the day, when I had walked along neglected wetlands near the Yakima River. On the banks, I absorbed smells that unleashed sensations and memories of the past, when I ventured into the deep sagebrush against my mother's wishes. Everywhere, the sacred spaces of my boyhood have become disfigured by trash and neglect. Old trails that I walked are now untended, left to survive on their own. The businesses I frequented have been shuttered.

And yet, I have to believe that things here have changed for the better. I must believe my perception of Yakima has been obscured by events in my youth and that I should recalibrate my lens. I must believe that there are parts of town that have been invigorated by good people who have dedicated themselves to the hard work of uplifting it. I am thankful to them for cultivating the spaces in which youth can emerge and thrive. But I still see poverty everywhere I look, and I can't help but be thrown by it.

Dawn comes down on this old land of mine as I weave, alone, under the same stars that I spent my life looking up at. I recall what I can of old times, trying to experience it in a way I couldn't fully absorb then and still am unable to now. I left so much behind. As I take in the sage-scented air, the weather-worn cars, I feel ashamed for letting these people go their own way without me. And yet the love, health, and happiness they live with didn't require my help to attain.

Yakima never needed me. I have to let it go—to let it live, thrive, die all on its own without me. I was only a minuscule instant in the long life of Yakima, and that moment has passed.

I drive back to my mother's home, where cracks in the pavement have burst under the intense heat. Alone in the backyard, I pull out my accordion.

I look back on this long journey of trailing my grandfather's ghost. I still struggle to capture his sound, to pull the tones from this instrument that would reconcile me to him. Then I stop, deflate the bellows, and slip the accordion back into its case, along with everything that I used to imagine my grandfather was.

It is not my place to try to mimic his playing anymore. I must find my own sound in the world I live in. I resolve to learn the next song, the very first one I heard coming out of a three-row Castagnari accordion: "Djevoujka." Massimo's powerful two-row interpretation of it seems achievable to me in a way it didn't before. And with that decision, I let go of my grandfather's spirit and set him free. I will no longer hound him for answers. My place is here and now. The only person I have to answer to is my boy who will one day, inevitably, judge me.

For too long, I've been embittered by a difficult past that ensnared me without my permission. For years, I have harnessed this bitterness as my strongest power. I fed off the hate that others had for me and my family and channeled it into a sickly energy source. It got me moving, kept me restless and uncomplacent. Hate lived on my shoulders and under my bed, a constant reminder to correct all the ways I have been wronged.

If I'm being honest with myself, hate has given me enormous strength. To a certain degree, I am thankful for the fire it has lit inside me. But it's an energy that no one should ever hold onto for that long. Eventually, it breaks the spirit. I've kept a firm grasp on it, too afraid of relinquishing the only power source I have. I'm afraid that if I let it go, I will have nothing to replace it with.

But I do my best to find other outlets. I seek the art in people's faces, in their singing and their playing, in picturesque landscapes. These, I know, are the things that will eventually free me from old wounds.

I sit here in silence, looking at my encased accordion, and think about the inevitable day when I too will be summoned from the spirit world to meet a grown man—my son, who will demand that I give him answers. I too will haunt the ground he steps on and I will stir as I try to make amends with him. I will be trapped in that realm of fathers who couldn't do enough for their children. I only hope that then, when we reconcile, my son will achieve peace.

I say to him here and now, "Summon me whenever. Call upon my spirit as often as you like. Give me no rest, even. Use me to breathe new life into your world, son. If music becomes your pursuit, allow me to embody it and give you breath and courage. May you one day forgive me for failing to be anything less than you wanted me to be."

—◆◆◆◆—

And with that, I close this corrido.

This code links to a playlist that features some of the accordionists in these pages. Bookended by exclusive compositions by Aaron Salinas, it also contains performances by Jeffery Broussard and Simone Bottasso.

ACKNOWLEDGMENTS

Mia: without her I could never have been a writer.

Rebecca Gradinger: who knew me back when I was a fledgling writer and who gives me the discipline to do my best work.

Tajja Isen: for her collaboration and for giving this book the life it really needed.

The good folk at Catapult: Lena, Nicole, and all the people in the background packaging books in warehouses somewhere.

To the musicians interviewed for this book:

Brother Broussard (Jeffrey), for holding his heart strongly in his hands, despite the bruises, and Millie. For the long days we shared on prairies lassoing stories that could heal us.

Aaron Salinas: for the enthusiasm he carries for his gente and for guiding me through his lands.

Ed Poullard: for sharing with me your accordion-building rituals. May your music and knowledge never be forgotten.

Simone Bottasso: for expecting the best of himself and of others through the experiment of music.

Will Pound: for digging deep about the dark things that sometimes afflict men. Peace to your heart.

Massimo Craveri: for feeling deeply and putting it on display for anyone to learn from. May we boldly embrace our emotions.

David Munnelly: for the folklore of his music and his words.

My grandfather: who ails in his tumultuous history. May his spirit have rest when it finally goes down. May there be mercy in his life in music.

Para mi primaso, H. Ya sabes quien eres, jefe. Saludos a ti y a tu rancho y a tu gente de por allá. Sin ti no se podría cantar este corrido. Muy agradecido de ti y por todo el esfuerza que le has echado. Ánimo hermano. Saludos y echale ganas.

Megha Majumdar: for seeing the fragments of something bigger and said yes.

Theo Nestor: for her endless love, support, and mentorship.

To the homies who are still hanging on and to the ones I had to let go of. To Jesus Castañeda, siempre el gran amigazo. De buena familia y de buen corazón. To Matt Magee. Stay real. Para el Pedro, siempre tirando pedrazos de poesías. Para el jugo del Hugo. To Ray man and Rachel. Grateful to be amongst some real Gs.

Castagnari accordions: for connecting me to their musicians. An incredible instrument to lay one's hands on. I'm honored to have started my accordion tradition with them.

Michael and the Concordia famiglia: for their enduring support.

To anyone I may have forgotten, don't let me forget it. Keep me accountable to all the things that matter in life. Life's too short to hold grudges.

To all those whom I have yet to cross paths with, and to the people who may not feel seen or heard: may you feel seen in this work. You too exist in these words. Here you are. Speak your pain through music. Give us your corridos.

NOÉ ÁLVAREZ is the author of *Spirit Run*. He was born in the desert and raised in the weeds.